ON MY BUCKET LIST

By

Sam W. McQuade

PREFACE

2018

I don't know the origin of the term, "Bucket List."

I know it is the name of a movie, starring Jack Nicholson and Morgan Freeman, which I have seen. But I think the movie is based on the idea of "Bucket List," which preceded the movie.

"Bucket List."

I rather like it.

And, as I grow older, I relate to it more and more.

If you are reading this, you relate.

The idea could only have been invented by a "Baby Boomer."

Because our Baby Boomer generation in America is the only one so far in all of history that has had the wealth, health, and leisure time in "the warm September of our years" to want to do things we have never done or visit places we have never seen.

I am a Baby Boomer, born in 1947, of two parents who both fought in WWII.

My father was a Master Technical Sergeant in the Marines, who was on the Fast Carrier, Bunker Hill, during the Battle of Okinawa that was attacked by two Kamikazes within some thirty seconds of one another, thereby putting it out of the war.

My mother was a Rosy Riveter in San Francisco while Dad was at sea.

I grew up in Bismarck, North Dakota, educated by Catholic nuns and priests in the 50s and 60s, graduated from Catholic St. John's University in Minnesota in 1969, following my junior year, '67-68, when I studied in Nantes, France, and met and fell in love with Maryvonne; we were married in December, 1968.

After obtaining an MA in Comparative Literature from Denver University, I was a professor of English and Humanities for three years at a community college in Denver. I found that I didn't really much like college professors, nor starving to death on an annual salary of $9,300, so I left teaching to work for Xerox in Denver, where I became the #5 salesman in a branch of 125, and tripled what I would have made as a college professor.

In 1975, my younger brother, Gerard, who was working for our Dad, with the goal of taking over our family beer distributorship in Bismarck, was killed in an auto accident in Montana.

Consequently, I returned to Bismarck.

While Maryvonne and I both felt we gave up a lot by making the decision to leave Denver for Bismarck, it has proved to be a good life. And one that has allowed us to travel extensively.

As I write this I have been to all 50 states and 41. foreign countries. I cannot tell you how many times we have returned to France. And we own a condo in Mazatlan, MX, where we now spend the winters.

I am now retired. Age: 71.

Not very happy about this…to be honest.

I would rather be 20, or 30, or 40, or 50, or 60…knowing what I know now.

But since that will never happen, I have a kind of "Bucket List" of things I want to do before I tip over.

The following are just a few that I have already completed.

CONDUCTING A SYMPHONY ORCHESTRA

I have no idea where this idea came from.

It actually happened February 4, 2017, when I conducted the Bismarck-Mandan Symphony Orchestra.

It most certainly did not happen because of my innate musical talents, or any musical education that I have had. Although one could say that I had an off-again, on-again musical education when I was young that continued into my mid-thirties.

Early Musical Education

My introduction to music occurred in the third grade at Cathedral Grade School in Bismarck, ND, with Sister Herman, who I remember as being tall with a mustache and facial hair. She was from the Germans from Russia area southeast of Bismarck, commonly referred to as "Iron Curtain Country" for the impenetrability of its inhabitants, mostly farmers. She spoke "Low German," the common language in Iron Curtain Country, much better than what English she could speak, the reason why we sang mostly songs in German: "Ich bin ein musikanter, Ich commen Schwabenland;" also that "Valderee, valdera…" song.

But there was one song we sang in English with a German accent we boys hated, because we had to stand next to our desks while singing and act it out:

It's going to be a long vinter,
Und vat vill da birdies do den,
Da poor tings?
Dey'll fly to da barn,
To keep demselves varm,
Und tuck der heads under der vings,
Da poor tings!

It was very embarrassing, even for third graders, to have to flap our arms and try to stick our heads under our armpits.

The Accordion

But not as embarrassing as the day Mom announced that my younger brother, Steve, and I would begin accordion lessons.

Learn to play the accordion!

Steve didn't seem to mind; he was a nerd before the word was invented.

But I hated the idea from the get-go. I begged. I pleaded with Mom. That I would pay for piano or guitar lessons from my own allowance.

To no avail.

Mom knew Lawrence Welk's success story backward and forward: born and raised on a farm near Strasburg, North Dakota, arguably the capital of "Iron Curtain Country," speaking only "Low German," (hence, his conducting the beginning of each song with "Ah von, und ah two..."), he learned to play the accordion, performing at German weddings with some oompah band, became famous because of the weekly Sunday television show, "The Champagne Music of Lawrence Welk," and now he owned half of Orange County, California.

Mom yelled at me, "Isn't that what you want to do?"

I didn't.

Especially if it required learning to play the accordion, which just has to be the hickest instrument ever invented. When Dad paid four hundred dollars – a fortune at the time -- for a garish red and white one I knew I was doomed to learn to play it.

Steve and I each had one-hour lessons every Saturday morning in the basement of Dahmer's Furniture Store on Main Street in Mandan, across the Missouri River from Bismarck. Dad drove us, and while we were getting our lessons, he would go to his favorite watering hole.

Dahmer's was straight out of Dickens' "Great Expectations." The basement was crammed with dining tables and chairs with complete table settings that hadn't been cleaned in years. The spider webs and dust were as thick as Dickens' description of Miss Haversham's jilted wedding reception.

Our accordion teacher was Wally Maki, a Finlander from the Iron Range in northern Minnesota. Wally had pitch-black hair cut with a stand-up flattop with heavily oiled slicked-back side fenders. Because his bowling team had its weekly competition just after our lessons, Wally always wore his shiny white silk bowling shirt with the sponsor's logo on the back and

"Wally" on the front. If you didn't already know him, from his appearance you might immediately assume Wally was the accordion player in a local oompah band.

Wally would wax eloquent about the accordion, which he called "an entire orchestra contained in one instrument." He pointed out the row of big buttons to the left of the keyboard on the right side. Push "G" for "General" (or something), and the accordion sounded like an accordion. Push any of the other buttons, and your accordion was instantly transformed into a clarinet, a violin, or a piccolo.

The Accordion Becomes a Piccolo

I discovered this the hard way when Mom insisted that Steve and I, after about a year of accordion lessons, participate in a talent show in the basement of the Cathedral Church. I remember about ten participants; I was to precede Steve on stage.

I had memorized my piece. Prior to walking on stage, I diligently kept pushing the "G" button to ensure my accordion sounded like an accordion.

But when I played the first note, it sounded like a piccolo.

Mortified with embarrassment, I stopped, pressed the "G" button, and played my short piece flawlessly.

Steve won the talent contest. I placed last.

At the start of eighth grade I told Mom I was going out for football, which left no time for daily accordion practice.

I have not touched one since. I hated the sound of it then. I hate the sound of it to this day.

I have no idea what became of Dad's four hundred dollar garish red and white accordion.

And I don't care.

Choir

While I hated the accordion I loved to sing in the choir, both in grade school, when I sang soprano, and in high school, when I was a tenor.

Not sure how much music or music theory I learned, because the director always announced the key and blew it on a kind of round harmonica. But I could follow the notes for my section.

Alas, my singing career was cut short in November my junior year in high school during wrestling practice. After practicing a bridging move with my head and neck to escape a pin hold, my throat felt like I was coming down with a cold. When I told the head coach about it he hit me in the face with his fist, yelling that I had

"...better be damned ready to wrestle in a tournament that weekend (that is how coaches toughened up kids in Catholic high school)."

After supper, while doing homework in my room, my throat felt like it was on fire; I figured I was coming down with Strep.

The next morning, while Dad was driving me to school, I told him I thought something was seriously wrong. He drove me to the hospital ER, where my throat was X-rayed and I was immediately checked into a room. Later the doc told me that I had cracked my trachea in three places, allowing air to seep into the cartilage. He said that if it didn't dissipate in three days, he would have to remove my voice box. I told him he would have to catch me first.

Eventually the air dissipated. So did my singing voice. I have never been able to "carry a note in a bucket" since.

Learning to Play the Piano at the Age of 30 +

Ironically, years later when I was in my early thirties, I had piano lessons for about five years.

I wanted ourtwo daughters, Shannon and Kelly, to learn to play the piano.

And I had always wanted to own a real, black grand piano (I don't know why exactly; I just liked the look of it); I had to take out a loan to purchase a Kimble 5'8" grand, so I decided to take piano lessons with them at Belle Mehus Conservatory of Music in Bismarck. The lessons took place in the basement of Belle's home; she lived on the floor above.

Belle was by then very elderly, a retired locally famous musical person, responsible for the successful musical careers of many young people.

I was not to be one of them.

Maybe because I was already too old when I started.

Royal Hopkins

What a wonderful name for a piano teacher!

Royal Hopkins was a brilliant pianist and organist. It was obvious from the outset that he wanted to make me into a concert pianist.

Alas.

It was not to be.

When I walked into his studio, he said, "Well, this is a red-letter day for me! A man in his thirties who wants to learn to play the piano. What prompted this?"

I explained the loan I had taken out to buy the grand piano, and that I wanted to learn to play it along with my daughters.

He asked me about my musical background. And I told him about the accordion lessons, and that I had sung in the school choir at Cathedral Grade School and St. Mary's High School.

He said, "Wonderful! What do you remember?"

I replied by hitting the key of "G," saying, "This is 'G.'"

He said, "Well this is a start."

Whereupon I stopped him cold.

Telling him that I was just a bit embarrassed to be beginning piano lessons at my age. That I would never participate in a piano recital with a bunch of little kids. And that if he ever hit my fingers with a ruler, I would promptly send him hurtling into the far wall.

He said, "Well, Sam! Now that we have the ground rules established, can we proceed?"

After some five years of lessons with Royal, and I did practice nearly every day, when I was able, I learned to play some pieces by Erik Satie and Frederick Chopin.

But at the end of one lesson we mutually decided to call it quits.

I really never learned to read music. But I could master a piece if I memorized it.

And from the first lesson Royal tried to explain to me the Circle of Fifths, apparently the most basic of music theory. I never understood it from the first lesson. And five years later, during an attempted review, I looked at Royal and said, "Royal, I have never understood the Circle of Fifths. I don't give a good goddamn about the Circle of Fifths. Can't you use the Suzuki method to train my fingers to play the notes?"

He said, "No."

So we parted ways.

The Idea for Conducting a Symphony Orchestra

It was sometime later that I had the idea that I wanted to conduct a symphony orchestra.

I think it happened on a Saturday, when I was channel surfing, and fell upon a program featuring Leonard Bernstein conducting the Berliner Philharmonic Orchestra in the fourth movement of Beethoven's Ninth Symphony, the Ode to Joy, based on the poem by Schiller.

If there exists more beautiful music than this, I am unaware of it.

At the end of the movement, Bernstein, sweat dripping from his forehead, brought the orchestra to a sudden halt with a baton thrust, slumped forward on the podium in obvious exhaustion, then rose to tumultuous applause and "bravos."

The thought struck me: what a way to go out!

Appropriately followed by a lightning strike to end my life in a blaze of glory.

Some years later the then Executive Director of the Bismarck-Mandan Symphony Orchestra called me at my office about making a contribution. I was just a little embarrassed when she reminded me that we had never contributed. We had never even attended a concert. It wasn't for a lack of interest; both my wife and I love symphonic music. I guess my excuse was that we were too busy raising our two daughters.

I invited her to talk about it in my office. She arrived accompanied by the young male conductor at the time. I had a movement of Henryk Gorecki's 3rd Symphony playing on my CD player, and he asked me, "What is that beautiful music?" I explained that I had discovered it by accident from an advertisement in "The New Yorker" magazine in a doctor's office. Gorecki began composing music rather late in his life; his 3rd Symphony, also called "Sorrowful Songs," was written as a memorial to the Holocaust.

The Challenge

I told them that I would fund a chair in the orchestra in exchange for the honor of conducting the Bismarck Mandan Symphony Orchestra.

Sans the lightning thing at the end.

Which solicited a big guffaw from the Executive Director and a much louder one from the conductor. I admit that I laughed also.

But I was serious.

So also were several of the Symphony board members when they somehow got word of it. I think for two reasons: one, it would be good PR; two, they probably thought they could get me to make a larger contribution.

Money talks.

But the young conductor objected, saying at a meeting of the Symphony Board of Directors, "If Sam McQuade can conduct the symphony orchestra, what do you need me for?"

About a year later they decided they didn't and fired him.

A New Chance?

Some years later I met the new, young female director, Beverly, at the Bismarck airport; we had been assigned adjacent seats on the flight to Minneapolis. While chatting I told her about my wish to conduct the symphony.

She seemed intrigued by the idea but was non-committal.

Although she did call me sometime later to invite me to a two-day symposium she was hosting on the art of conducting at Bismarck State College.

A number of Bismarck-Mandan Symphony board members were in attendance; they all laughed when I announced the reason I was there: that I wanted to conduct the orchestra.

I didn't think the idea was all that far-fetched.

I learned from friends and business acquaintances that much larger symphony orchestras routinely auction off the privilege to amateurs at donor banquets. Typically it involves conducting "Sleigh Ride" or some such fluff at the lighter holiday concert.

I wanted to do something more serious.

Then It Happened

Then it happened.

In July, 2016, a friend, who is now on the Bismarck-Mandan Symphony Orchestra Board of Directors, informed me that a new

Executive Director had been hired, and that somehow she had gotten word of my bucket list desire. She had told him, "You tell Sam that there is a new sheriff in town, and if he is serious about contributing the sum I have heard mentioned, we'll make it happen."

Money talks.

My friend made dinner reservations at a Bismarck restaurant, where Beverly, the conductor, seated to my right, cut to the chase: what piece did I have in mind? I told her two: Leonard Bernstein's First Symphony, "Jeremiah," second movement; or Dimitri Shostakovich's Eighth Symphony, third movement.

I had them downloaded on my IPhone and had memorized both.

She shook her head.

I asked why.

She said, "Sam, I admire your taste in classical music, but our Symphony Orchestra musicians are volunteers and not very numerous. We simply don't have the horsepower to do justice to those pieces."

Although I am not certain she used the word, "horsepower."

I asked her what she had in mind, and she said, "How about the Finale to Igor Stravinsky's "Firebird Ballet?"

Which I have always liked for its fiery ending.

So it was agreed. We made an appointment to meet in my office to go over the score.

I must admit that when she walked me through the orchestral score as we listened to a rendition on my CD player it looked to me like pages of Chinese letters, and immediately I got cold feet.

Oh, Shit!

Be careful what you wish for; it might happen.

In a state of panic, I said, "Maybe this isn't such a good idea."

She said, "You will do just fine. It will be great!"

For about an hour we rehearsed together the right hand conducting movement of the Finale's three beat measure.

At least that is what Beverly said it was. I would never have known myself. She did it so naturally and gracefully, while I struggled to follow her.

Finally, I kind of got it.

With that she got up to leave, told me to practice as often as I could, and suggested another appointment about a month hence when she would bring an electronic keyboard to play the Finale while watching me conduct.

At that moment I realized I had made a big mistake by shooting my mouth off about wanting to conduct a serious piece of music with a symphony orchestra.

Just who the hell did I think I was? Leonard Bernstein? I was merely a retired beer peddler.

Was it too late to request a performance of "Sleigh Ride?"

The Light at the End of the Tunnel

After several frustrating days of trying to follow the musical score of the Finale to the rendition on my CD player, while attempting to conduct it with the three beat hand movement Beverly had shown me, I gave up. I just knew I was going to get booed by the audience at the February concert.

All I could think of was what one of the French Horn musicians in the Bismarck Orchestra had told me: "Conducting is far more complicated than it looks; you cannot simply stand in front of an orchestra gesticulating wildly; it must be led, and, in order to lead, the conductor must know the piece by heart."

That was it!

I needed to memorize the entire Finale, all four minutes of it!

Forget the score!

Which I couldn't read anyway.

I Googled the Finale on my office computer and found a number of videos featuring various conductors and orchestras, including two videos of Stravinsky himself. Which really confused me: he wasn't conducting with anything like a three beat measure; he was gesticulating wildly. So, it appeared to me, did the other conductors.

I emailed Beverly about what I had discovered. She replied, "Yeah. You can pretty much do whatever you want. Just get the downbeats right."

So I began to practice conducting to the video version of the Finale by Russian conductor, Valery Gergiev, leading the Vienna Philharmonic Orchestra. Not his conducting style, which seemed to me to be nothing less than nonsensical wild gesticulating. But I liked his interpretation more than any of the others I had found, especially the final note, which he has the orchestra hold for some twenty seconds. An eternity, as I found out later, for certain musicians in the orchestra.

Leopold!

Have you ever seen the Bugs Bunny cartoon, titled, "Opera Singer?"

Bugs is awakened in his hole by the vocal exercises of a male opera singer, and he is none too happy about it; he declares, "Of course, this means war!'

So Bugs shows up at the Hollywood Bowl, dressed in a tuxedo and a long, white wig, walks through the orchestra, to exclamations, "It is Leopold!" Presumably based on the real life symphony conductor, Leopold Stokowski, who was well known for his irascibility and zero tolerance for mistakes, and proceeds to get revenge on the poor opera singer by putting him through a conductor's wringer.

Imitating Bugs, I also decided to grow my hair long.

If I couldn't be a real conductor, at least I could look like one.

Beverly arrived a month later at my office without the electronic keyboard, reassuring me that I would do just fine. I wasn't so sure.

But I felt a lot better about my prospects after she watched me conduct to the video of Valery Gergiev that I was following in my practices.

Determined that I was not going to screw up my one chance at symphonic fame, or worse, make myself out to be an idiot in front of the audience in the Belle Mehus Auditorium in Bismarck, I practiced conducting the Finale daily for the next five and a half months. Many days I practiced it multiple times.

I could do it in my sleep.

What I Had Wished For Was About to Happen

My wife, Maryvonne, and I returned to Bismarck from our winter condo in Mazatlan, Mexico, a week before the concert on Saturday, February 4, 2017. Three practices were scheduled on Tuesday, Thursday, and Friday.

Not only was I determined not to screw up this one chance at symphonic fame, I wanted to do it right by thanking the musicians for their going along with my crazy bucket list wish with a catered beer and wine post-concert party.

The conducting "fee" and the party would total $7,500. Not included: tuxedo rental.

Maryvonne said, "This will be the most expensive four minutes of your life."

I said, "I don't care. It will only happen once."

On Tuesday, although I was scheduled on the program to conduct just before Intermission, I was first up for practice.

I hadn't been nervous in the least until the moment I stepped up to the director's podium. A sea of faces greeted me; behind them was a single question: what the hell is this guy doing here?

At that moment I had the same question: "What the hell am I doing here?"

But it was too late to flee.

So I raised my right hand to the solo French Horn musician who would begin the Finale, and began the three beat measure.

Four minutes later, as I excitedly gesticulated to the Orchestra to lengthen the final note to twenty seconds, I was nearly knocked off the podium by the blast of sound blowing at me.

After I closed with a final hand thrust, I looked at the musicians and said, "Wow! I could really get used to this!"

But they knew and I knew that I only had this one chance.

This was my one shot.

Beverly, the real conductor, had been sitting on a folding chair behind the Orchestra.

When I finished, she jumped out of her chair and charged the podium.

I just knew I had done something horribly wrong and she was going to give me both barrels.

Instead she said, "Sam! If everyone in Bismarck showed the same passion for classical music you just demonstrated, we would never have a problem with fund-raising!"

I nearly collapsed from relief.

We rehearsed the Finale several more times that night.

After one run-through I asked Everaldo, the cool pony-tailed Concert Master, the First Violinist, if I had held the final note for twenty seconds, as I intended.

He said, "How would I know? Sam, you don't have to count."

I said, "I don't?"

He said, "No. Just look at the brass players, especially the Tuba player (an elderly gentleman); when their faces turn purple, that's when you need to shut us down."

I think it was after the rehearsal on Thursday that the young timpanist told me, "Sam! We just love the way you conduct! The more passion you show the better we will perform! So, ham it up!"

I assured him I didn't think I would have a problem with that.

And I didn't.

Conducting the Finale of Igor Stravinsky's "Firebird Ballet"

In spite of the cold February weather the Belle Mehus Auditorium was nearly full for the Saturday concert. The Symphony Executive Director said that many attendees were there because I was on the program.

Although our family is well known in Bismarck -- big fish, small pond -- I rather doubted that. But, if true, they probably expected me to fall on my face.

And were there to witness it.

After all, who in the hell did I think I was? Leonard Bernstein? Most of those in attendance who knew me only knew me as a retired beer peddler.

A lady musician backstage asked me if I was nervous.

I told her truthfully, "No, I am not. I probably should be. But I have practiced for more than five months. If I screw this up now, shame on me."

Reassuringly, she said, "Well, you haven't screwed up in practice. Good luck, just the same!"

Before going on stage I asked the Executive Director how Igor Stravinsky's "Firebird Ballet"

Finale fit in that concert's theme: "Celtic Connections." She said, "It doesn't. We're just doing this for you and the money."

With that, the stage grip held me back to allow Beverly to exit the podium after conducting her last piece.

She gave me a wink as she passed.

I had been told to go on stage, bow to the audience, shake the hand of Everaldo, the Concert Master, mount the podium, and pause while the Orchestra prepared to play the Finale.

With my right hand raised, I was then to begin the three beat measure for the solo French Horn player.

After the final note, I was told to signal the entire Orchestra to rise and bow, acknowledge the French Horn soloist, descend the podium, shake Everaldo's hand, bow to the audience, and exit stage right.

Which I did.

The stage grip said, "Sam, you need to go back on stage for more bows."

I admit at that point I was as nervous as I had ever been.

I asked, "Why?"

"Can't you hear? The audience is giving you a standing ovation."

I said, "That can't be for me. It's for the Orchestra's performance."

"No, it's for you! Get out there now!"

I walked back on stage to people standing, applauding, shouting "Bravo!"

It actually was for me!

I found it to be unreal. All I could do was raise my arms in a kind of shrug.

While thinking, "I could really get used to this."

But knowing that this was my only shot.

What an experience!

One of the very best of my life! Maybe the ultimate on my "Bucket List."

And the best part? When I was mobbed by my three grandchildren, identical twin girls, eighteen, and my fourteen year old grandson. They all said, "Papa Sam, you were awesome!'

"Awesome!"

DRIVING A PORSCHE 150 MPH
ON A GERMAN AUTOBAHN

This happened on a Sunday afternoon in May, 2017, when our group of nine in five Porsches, left our hotel in Stuttgart, Germany, for a five day Porsche driving adventure, with a guarantee that we would join the "150MPH Club," promised by Fast Lane Travel out of Florida.

I was solo, assigned a new Porsche 911 4 S, four-wheel drive, capable of 195 MPH, which I was hoping to achieve on a German Autobahn, sections of which have no speed limits, clearly marked.

Our lead driver, Peter, owner of Fast Lane Travel, assured us in a three-hour briefing the day before, that we would be perfectly safe...as long as we followed his lead, and we knew the rules of driving in Germany.

His introduction was rather ominous: "To obtain a driver's license in Germany is the equivalent to obtaining a pilot's license in the US. It requires months, if not years, and not everyone qualifies. You certainly do not qualify with your licenses issued by your individual US states; therefore we will provide each vehicle with a walkie-talkie, so that I can keep you from violating any rules."

"The most important rule is No Alcohol at any time when you are driving! There are virtually no DUI offenses in Germany or Austria for good reason: your car is confiscated and you go to jail. There is no plea bargaining as exists in the States."

With that warning ringing in our ears, he said he looked forward to accompanying us to the Stuttgart Spring "Oktoberfest" that evening in a big beer hall (we wouldn't be driving).

Following the meeting I asked Peter what could we expect at the beer hall.

He told me, "It will be loud, crowded, smoky (in spite of the laws against smoking in public), with lots of drunken Germans, a couple of whom will puke on your shoes."

I decided to pass.

But I did see Peter in the hotel lobby prior to the group's departure to the beer hall, in full German leather lieder hosen and one of those goofy German hats with the pheasant tail; I told him I thought he looked perfectly ridiculous.

And he did.

Which didn't seem to bother him in the least (he was born in Austria).

The next day was Sunday, when our group was to leave Stuttgart to venture onto a four lane-wide (in one direction) German Autobahn, many sections with no speed limit, so we could easily join the 150 MPH Club.

Moreover Peter had informed us that Germany does not allow any truck traffic on its autobahns on Sunday, so we would have the road to ourselves, except for the other crazies trying to join their own personal 150 MPH Club.

During our orientation Peter pointed out that on every Porsche Driving Adventure, American drivers automatically hit the brakes when they see a patrol car. He advised against doing so, saying, "Speed up to pass the patrol car; the cop will appreciate your aggressiveness by waving to you!"

He also said, "No snickering on the walkie-talkie when you see 'Ausfahrt;' it means 'Exit.'"

I was hoping to max out my Porsche at 195 MPH.

I had already achieved 150 MPH plus on a closed road circuit at Le Mans, France, a couple of years before.

150 MPH might not seem very fast, compared to the speeds achieved by NASCAR and INDY and FORMULA ONE cars.

But just try it sometime.

The white stripes zip by in a hurry you have never imagined.

That Sunday in Stuttgart we left the parking lot of the hotel in a rain, at times a downpour. It rained off and on all the way to our destination in Austria, which, sensibly, has speed limits on its autobahns.

Following Peter, driving a Porsche Panamera 4 S, a four-wheel drive sedan, I hit 245 KPH, 150 MPH +, four times...in the rain.

I have never felt my sphincter pucker like it did.

I cannot say that it was exhilarating.

But it probably was.

I like to consider myself fearless in the face of danger, but 150 MPH in the rain, even in a four-wheel drive Porsche, instantly reminded me that I was 70 years old, and had NO business doing what I was doing.

My fragile mortality also loomed very large.

I have to believe we were close to hydroplaning the tires.

I don't know that.

I don't really want to know.

I am now a four-time official member of the 150 MPH Club, and have the certificate and the shirt to prove it.

So, there!

The days that followed, I began to quickly realize that there was no chance to max out my Porsche at 195 MPH.

That Sunday, had it been dry, was the only opportunity, as the rest of our driving was on tortuous mountain roads or on two-lane autobahns with solid semi-truck traffic in the right lane.

Even in the "No Speed Limit" sections, it was dangerous to exceed 120-130 MPH, as, at any given moment, a car trailing behind a semi would put on its blinkers to pass, forcing me (us) to dynamite our brakes. Several times I pulled into rest stops with my disc brakes smoking.

It was the two-lane, snaking mountain roads that proved to be a blast.

With Peter as lead blocker, constantly barking instructions via his walkie-talkie to the rest of us: "Clear, clear, speed up! Car coming! Red Audi! Clear, clear, let's go! Slowdown! Truck! Now past! Clear! Let's go..."

We were able to drive the "racing line" of the road, rather than cling to the right.

What fun! In fact, better than getting close to hydroplaning tires at 150 MPH.

German and Austrian Rest Stops

In the US we call them "Truck Stops." Generally they are horrible, filthy, overcrowded joints, with unclean bathrooms and fast food restos that serve shitty food.

We may be #1 in a lot of things, but the category, rest stops, is not one of them.

Not so in Germany and Austria. Their rest stops are just that: an oasis off the autobahn, designed for enjoyment and relaxation, a respite from driving.

As I entered our first rest stop I halted in my tracks in the entryway: there, on the floor, was a dish of clean water and a dish of kibbles marked: "For Fido."

Use of the bathroom will cost you half a Euro, but one doesn't mind, as it is spotless and doesn't stink.

Hungry? Choose from a variety of snacks to go, or have a leisurely lunch from a buffet of kaleidoscopic gourmet choices.

Thirsty? There is a coffee and juice stand. And one can even purchase beer, wine, and alcohol...for passengers only.

Our Porsche Driving Adventure

Over the next four nights we stayed in wonderful accommodations before our return to Stuttgart: a hotel on a lake near Mad Ludwig's castle in southern

Bavaria, which Peter discouraged us from visiting, unless we enjoyed being mobbed by Japanese tourists with cameras; two nights in a wonderful Austrian alpine resort; and one night in Munich.

Mostly we enjoyed wonderful breakfasts. But only a couple of lunches and dinners that I would describe as passably "enjoyable;" read: "edible."

I have this theory that the German people are the way they are…because they eat the most abominable food in all of Europe: nothing that doesn't come in an animal casing.

The reason why they were at war with their neighboring countries from the time of Bismarck until the fall of Hitler's Third Reich, May, 1945, one hundred years, give or take? Their soldiers were guarding their borders wearing those heavy pickelhaube (spear-pointed) helmets, while sniffing, "What the hell are they cooking over there?"

That is my theory. And I am sticking with it until convinced otherwise, which is unlikely to happen.

On this trip the only time I might have been persuaded to change my opinion was at a wonderful Austrian restaurant, next to a mountain stream, that served fresh trout for lunch.

All the rest of the food was Teutonic offal.

At our five star mountain resort in Austria, Peter highly recommended the Wienerschnitzel, supposedly their specialty.

I passed, ordering a soup and dessert.

Wienerschnitzel is a plate of veal. Which should be wonderful itself: tender and flavorful.

But not to the Hun.

Who likes his veal pounded flat into about a half-inch high serving, covered with about three inches of batter, deep-fried, and served with sauerkraut and potatoes.

The guy sitting next to me could hardly cut it.

He made me sick just watching him trying to eat it.

And he never finished it.

Other than the restaurant in Austria that served the fresh trout from the adjacent stream, the best restaurant I found was an Asian restaurant in Stuttgart.

The Porsche Factory in Stuttgart, 1967

I was at the Porsche Factory in December, 1967, to pick up my first Porsche, a 912: 911 body with the Ferdinand Porsche air-cooled, flat-four cylinder engine, that produced 115 HP, with a top-end of 115 MPH. Cost: $4,125 US.

It was the cheapest Porsche available.

I wanted to buy a Porsche 911 T, L, or S: six cylinder models with more horsepower, but I had saved only about $3,000 working for Dad as summer help in our family beer distributorship, and I didn't feel right asking him to kick in a bigger difference, even if he could have afforded it at the time.

$4125 was on the high-end of what vehicles cost back then. But Dad was spending $3,000 + for Buicks.

It is not like the price differential today, when a 911 Porsche Turbo S costs $200,000.

But that is not a fair comparison.

A new Porsche 911 Turbo S produces 610 HP in Sport Plus Mode, is four-wheel drive, with computerized torque control to all four wheels, and has four-wheel steer. 0-60 in 2.8 seconds. Top end: 205 MPH.

In 1967 no such car existed at any price.

Anyway, my friend, Dan, a fellow student of our group, studying our junior year at the Institute of European Studies, in Nantes, France, and I arrived in Stuttgart a few days before Christmas, 1967, to take possession of my new Porsche 912.

We were then bound for Lermoos, Austria, for two weeks of skiing, staying in an Austrian Gasthaus through a French student organization. Cost: $120 US for room and three square meals per day.

Beer, schnapps and ski tickets not included.

But a quart of beer cost 30 cents US, as did a glass of schnapps; a punch ski ticket cost about $5.00; if you skied your ass off, the ticket was good for about 2 ½ days.

Dan and I arrived at the Stuttgart train station in early evening. We needed to find a place to sleep, and we were hungry.

We found a cheap hotel. And after passing by a number of smoky beer halls (neither of us smoked), we gave up and entered one.

A buxom Frau waitress gave us menus, which were in German, which we didn't understand, and, in German, asked us (I guessed) what we wanted to order. When we responded first in American English, which she didn't understand, much less our French, in German she yelled at us something about we were now in Germany, and we needed to speak German. At least I think that is what she yelled.

In English I tried to remind her that her country lost the last two world wars.

But if fell on uncomprehending ears (probably a good thing!).

So, for Dan and me, I ordered the only food I knew how to pronounce in German: "Bratwurst und bier!"

Which we were served along with sauerkraut, potatoes, and bread, which I think in German, are: sauerkraut, kertoffal, und brot.

The next day we took a cab to the Porsche factory.

After presenting my ID at the front desk, we were asked to take a seat; a guide would arrive shortly to give us a factory tour.

Which was fascinating.

Nothing was automated. No robots. Only humans.

Humans were everywhere: moving 911 bodies on tracks in the ceiling; building engines; hand-rubbing the latest coat of paint on a 911 body, teams installing interiors…

And all the workers were drinking beer from what looked like Mason jars.

I asked our guide, "What the hell is going on here?"

He said, "Oh, the beer? Well Christmas vacation is just a couple of days away, so we're letting the workers get a little jump start"

I said, "Well good for them!"

Then I asked, "When was my car built?"

He said, "Don't worry. About three weeks ago."

After the factory tour Dan and I were led into an office, next to a drive-through garage. I assumed my Porsche would be driven there and someone would walk me through a review of its systems and, especially, the break-in protocol.

We waited for minutes.

Finally a young man in a suit and tie entered the office; he appeared to be in his late twenties.

He asked, "Which of you is Sam McQuade?"

Whereupon I rose from my seat.

He gave me the longest Teutonic stare, appraising me from top to bottom.

It was very disconcerting, because I had no idea who he was or why he was questioning me.

He asked, "How old are you?"

I answered honestly, "I am 20; I will be 21 in April."

He demanded: "Do you have any idea how many Germans can afford a Porsche that you are about to take possession of?"

(Remember this was December, 1967, only 22 years after the German Unconditional Surrender.

Bombed parts of Stuttgart had not yet been repaired).

I tried my very best, for once, to be diplomatic. I said, "Sir. I have no idea."

He shouted in my face, "NOBODY!"

The only thing missing was his right-hand Nazi salute.

I wanted to remind this Kraut asshole that his country had lost the last two world wars.

I was very tempted.

It would have been completely appropriate. After all, I was HIS CUSTOMER, no matter what my age.

But I didn't.

After that Dan and I couldn't wait to get the hell out of the Porsche factory to begin our drive to Lermoos, Austria.

Porsche Museum and Factory Tour, May, 2017

Not quite 50 years later, the Porsche people were far more accommodating and friendlier than the former Hitler Youth Dan and I encountered in December, 1967.

A good thing.

And for a good reason: Porsche models in '67-68 were expensive; now they are priced far above comparable makes and models.

With one caveat: Porsche makes the best cars in the world, no matter the model, no matter the price.

Period.

The day before the tour our Porsche Driving Adventure group returned to our hotel in Stuttgart for a farewell dinner in a German restaurant, serving "German

Cuisine" which had become to me by then an oxymoron.

The next day we were driven to the Porsche Museum and a factory tour in the suburb of Zuffenhausen.

When I toured the Porsche factory in December, 1967, and picked up my Porsche 912, there was no museum.

Now there is a world-class museum across the intersection from the factory; our group was allowed over two hours before lunch in the museum cafeteria to gawk at Porsches from original 365s to LMP1s (prototypes) that had recently won the 24 Hours of Le Mans.

I was most pleased to find a 1968 Porsche 912, exactly the same car, except for its navy blue color, as the Porsche I had picked up at the factory in December, 1967.

Made me wonder whatever happened to the neo-Nazi PR guy who had confronted me then.

Following lunch our group got a two and one-half hour tour of the Stuttgart factory, which produces 250 911s, 718s (formerly the Cayman), and Boxters daily.

A conservative estimate: more than $22,000,000 per day!

The Panamera (four-door sedan), Cayenne and Macan SUVs are built in the city of Leipzig. Our guide didn't know the daily output of that factory. But the Macan is currently the most purchased Porsche in the US, at about $60,000 per car.

Do the math.

And our young guide said that the US was formerly Porsche's most important market, now surpassed by China. He told us rich Chinese housewives buy up Porsche Boxters as fast as they are built.

The factory tour was fascinating.

As I wrote, on my tour in December, 1967, automation simply didn't exist: everything, including pushing bodies from one station to the next, was all done by hand, until the car was finished.

The only differences I noted on this tour: 1) bodies now move on automated platforms from one station to the next; 2) we saw a few, but only a few robots, which, it was explained, only perform repetitive tasks (turning screws) that would drive a human crazy; 3) workers are divided into teams: every few weeks a team is shifted to another part of the assembly line, so they don't get bored, and they eventually learn how to assemble complete Porsche models.

Everything else is accomplished by hand. So the Porsche you buy is really a hand-built vehicle.

The engines are assembled by hand in a separate building.

All parts of a new vehicle arrive "just in time" on the assembly line by robotic delivery vehicles that follow lines on the factory floor. Kind of like the hallways of the spaceships in "Star Wars."

Our guide took us to the interior department; I thought this would be boring, but it turned out to be the most interesting thing we saw on the entire tour.

He explained that the leather interior of a Porsche 911, 718, or Boxter requires the hides of three bulls (not cows), as bull hides are more robust. And the hides come from bulls raised on one ranch in Texas.

We entered one room where mostly women were stitching the hides on machines; in the next area we saw several men hand-molding the stitched leather to the aluminum forms of dashboards.

I own a Porsche 911 Turbo S and a Cayenne Turbo: the leatherwork with its immaculate stitching is flawless, a work of art.

By the end of the tour, I was reminded of what our trip leader, Peter, had told us before he left to return to Florida: "You are going to witness German efficiency and perfection personified."

Then he asked if any one of us had ever toured the Ferrari factory in Italy; none of us had. Peter said we should do it sometime after touring the Porsche factory. He said, "At Ferrari, there is little to no efficiency and no "just–in-time" delivery of parts. Only one Italian who yells to his fellow worker, "Hey-a, Luigi, you gotta this-a part?"

Nurburgring

When booking the Porsche Driving Adventure out of Stuttgart, Sven, of Fast Lane Travel, had encouraged me to extend my tour with a drive in a rental car to the famous racetrack in Nurburging in northwest Germany for an initial hot-lap in a Porsche GT3 with a professional driver, followed by my driving six laps in a Porsche Cayman, set up for racing, with another professional race driver, who would be my safety instructor.

If you are ever presented with such an opportunity by anyone to race on the Nurburgring, respond with an emphatic, "NEIN!"

Then run like hell!

In my seventy years on this Earth I have never done anything this dangerous.

Let me explain.

The Nurburgring might be the most famous racetrack of them all. But known mostly only to Germans and Europeans

It is also one of the deadliest, if not the deadliest, of all racetracks. It kills on average 3-12 non-professional drivers per year; 72 professional race drivers have died on it; YouTube has recorded more than 7,000 crashes.

Want to have a good time/laugh at the expense of others? Google YouTube Nurburgring Crashes.

It is a monster: 12.9 miles of road circuit, 73 corners, about 80% of them blind, with a 1,000 foot elevation change.

Jackie Stewart, arguably the greatest race driver ever, called it "The Green Hell."

But none of this stops the crazies, the wanna-be Jackie Stewarts.

My safety driver, Michael, whose team won the 24 Hours of Nurburgring in the early nineties, told me that anyone with 30 Euros in his pocket is allowed to race any kind of car. He said, "Ninety-five plus per cent of them haven't a clue what they are doing." Even more forbidding: "On any Sunday with good weather, upwards of five-hundred cars of all kinds of performance capabilities can be on the track at the same time!"

After a night in a hotel in the medieval town of Nurburg, the first stop of my Nurburgring experience was the office of Rent4Ring, where my credit card was swiped to the tune of $30,000 Euros (about $33,000 US) as a damage deposit on the Porsche Cayman I would be driving. Michael, a tall, gray-haired German, in his late 50s-early 60s, I guessed, introduced himself. We then got in the Cayman and Michael drove us to the Rent4Ring parking area and tent near the Nurburgring start line.

Michael introduced me to another driver, a German, forget his name, so I'll call him Fritz, who, in spite of his smoking, was obviously a workout buff, as his arms bulged with bicep muscles. He was to be the race driver of a Porsche GT3 for my hot lap.

As we waited for the track to open he asked me what, if any kind, of racing experience I had. I told him that I had been to four Porsche Driving Schools in the last three years, three at a track in Birmingham, and one at a closed circuit in Le Mans, France. I explained that at my last three-day school in Birmingham, I obtained my license to race on SCCA courses in the States.

I thought he would be duly impressed.

He wasn't.

I soon found out why.

I think most boys growing up imagine that they have the skills to be a race driver. For many, this carries on into manhood, especially if one can afford a sports car.

That certainly describes me; I have owned four Porsche sports cars in my life: the 912 I bought at the Stuttgart factory in December, 1967, a 2012 911 Carrera S, a 2015 911 Turbo, and a 2017 911 Turbo S.

It was the dealer in Fargo, ND, who encouraged me to learn to drive the 911s by attending Porsche Driving Schools.

Fritz swiped his credit card from his window to pay for the hot lap, and positioned the GT3 in line for the start. As soon as the flag dropped he accelerated rapidly, controlling the gears with the steering wheel paddles. The cars that had preceded us were easily overtaken as if they were standing still, and I began to get just a bit queasy from the G Forces we pulled around the corners. Fritz kept asking, "You ok?" I could only nod, as I doubt he could have heard me over the roar of the engine.

At one point, going over a low rise, the GT3 went air-borne.

At the place on the track where spectators are allowed to sit on the side of a hill, protected from crash debris only by a steel mesh fence, we caught up to a yellow Mustang convertible, the driver of which was occupied with trying to pass slower cars in front of him, so, consequently, blocked us from passing. Finally Fritz spotted an opening and we passed the Mustang as if it had been standing still.

When we crossed the finish line, Fritz slowed and asked me what I thought.

All that came out was, "Holy Shit!"

We had done a lap of the Nurburgring in under eight minutes. The record is just under seven. We would have had a better time had it not been for the Mustang. I asked Fritz our top speed, and he replied, "At least 170 MPH."

I couldn't begin to imagine what it would take to drive a racecar at those speeds and constant Gs for an entire race. No wonder race drivers are mostly young!

Back at Rent4Ring parking I begged Michael for a bit of time to recuperate from the hot lap with Fritz before driving my own laps.

When I was finally ready I drove the Cayman for two laps, passing many cars, but also being passed by a number. Michael, in the passenger seat, warned me about the severity of each upcoming corner, where and how much to brake, and when and where and how much to accelerate.

After the two laps Michael suggested a break in a café adjacent to the Rent4Ring tent. Over a cup of coffee he told me it was obvious I knew how to drive a racecar, but that a mere six laps would not be nearly enough to learn the nuances of the Nurburgring. In his career and retirement from competitive racing, he figured he had driven a minimum of 30,000 laps.

I told him that I agreed completely, as it had taken me until the very last hot lap at the third Porsche Driving School in Birmingham, AL, before I felt that I had finally mastered the Barber road circuit, which is only 2.4 miles in length.

While on our break we heard loud thunder, followed by a huge cloudburst of rain that closed the track for more than an hour.

When we heard the announcement that the track had reopened, Michael said, "Well, let's see how you race on a wet track."

Whereupon I stopped him cold, telling him that there was no way I was going to risk $33,000 simply to brag that I had driven the Nurburgring after a cloudburst of biblical proportions. I asked if he was insured by Rent4Ring if the Cayman was damaged. When he replied that he was insured, I said, "I have a better idea: you do a couple of laps to show me how to properly drive on a wet track."

He called it the "wet line," as opposed to the "racing line" of a dry track. We passed every car we met. There was standing water everywhere, and the Cayman was much "squirlier" than when I had driven it, skidding a bit through the tighter corners.

We passed a wrecker truck, which I thought curious.

Then we met our first wreck. A guy was standing in front of a new or newer red Audi that was pretty much totaled; he had his head in both hands.

I asked Michael, "What's that guy's insurance company going to say when he submits the claim for his wreck?"

Michael said, "He won't. No one can buy insurance to race a car on the Nurburgring. That is why you paid a 30,000 Euro damage deposit. He will have to pay the cost of the repairs, or buy another car. He will also have to pay the cost of the wrecker we just passed and for any damage he did to the track or the barriers. I'm guessing that the reason his head is in his hands is that he is wondering how he is going to explain how he wrecked the family car to his missus!"

I was astounded.

We passed a couple more wrecked cars and a sports car that had its rear bumper waving back and forth, nearly torn off; obviously it had slid backward into a barrier.

By far the most cars on the track that day were Opel station wagons and various makes of SUVs, vehicles not designed to produce down force. Watch a couple of YouTube Nurburgring videos;

most of the crashes involve family cars that have no business being raced...even by professionals. The flat bottom chassis sends the cars air-borne, the driver loses any control, and becomes simply a passenger on a roller-coaster run amok.

One YouTube video I saw showed a car flying vertically about six feet in the air, crashing into the flimsy steel mesh fence in front of that hill of spectators. I don't know what happened to that driver, but am guessing he became one of those annual 3-12 non-professional Nurburgring fatalities.

After Michael's two wet laps, the track dried; I drove another lap, then had Michael drive a hot lap, which was mild compared to the one with Fritz, which I attributed to the difference in the performance of the GT3 versus the Cayman.

Back at the Rent4Ring office my credit card receipt for the $33,000 US damage deposit was handed back to me; I immediately tore it up and dropped the shreds into a wastebasket.

Michael shook my hand, thanking me for my coming…and for not killing him on the track. He said, "I enjoyed driving with you, and hope you return another time."

I thanked him in turn, but told him that a return was "highly doubtful."

I will never return to drive the Nurburgring.

Are you kidding me?

REFIGHTING WWII IN THE EUROPEAN THEATER

"The Rise and Fall of Hitler's Germany" Tour with the New Orleans WWII Museum

First, a bit of background.

My father, who became known as Sam McQuade Sr, I guess because most knew me as Sam McQuade Jr., even though that is not my legal name, nor is "Sr." his, joined the Marine Corps in June, 1942, in, of all places, Butte, Montana. Because he just happened to be there as a salesman for Grain Belt Beer, brewed by Minneapolis Brewing Co., in what was called Nordeast, Minneapolis, populated by mostly Polish who had emigrated over many years.

But Dad was from Virginia, Minnesota, at the eastern edge of the Iron Range in northern, Minnesota.

Much later I learned to take almost anything Dad told me with a big grain of salt.

He was the ultimate bullshitter.

He told me he lied his age during the interview at Grain Belt for a sales job, claiming he was the minimum age of 21, when, in reality, he was younger.

I will never know the truth.

But he was hired, and spent the years before the attack on Pearl Harbor, December 7, 1941, traveling the Dakotas, Montana, Idaho, and the state of Washington with an irascible Grain-Belt old-timer by the name of Joe Kelly, whom Dad chose as my godfather, when I was born April 8, 1947, after the war.

The only thing I know about Joe was when Mom, years later, described his reaction on first seeing me as a newborn. Mom asked him which parent I most resembled; he said, "He don't look like nothing."

As to Dad and his stint in the Marines Corps in WWII...I will get to that in the next chapter, "Victory in the Pacific," with the WWII Museum in New Orleans.

Dad got me started on an obsession with, first, WWII in the Pacific, when he gave me a copy of a book titled, "History of Marine Corps Aviation in WWII."

I now have an entire library of books about WWII in the Pacific, the European Theater, and the Holocaust.

If you study WWII, that inevitably leads to a study of WWI, which, in turn leads to the American Civil War, which leads back to the Napoleonic Wars.

Why?

Because, it is my observation, that throughout history generals always fight the last war, employing the same battle tactics, but what has changed every time is the advance in weaponry. It has always taken generals far too long to realize the change and adapt.

Napoleon had smooth bore cannon; the American Civil war had rifled cannons and the Minie ball; WWI saw massive artillery and machine guns; WWII saw fast moving tanks and attack planes and bombers.

The WWII Museum in New Orleans

The museum was first opened on June 6, 2006, a collaboration between the famous author/historian, Stephen Ambrose, and a colleague at the University of New Orleans, Gordon Mueller.

When I first learned about the location of the museum, New Orleans, I was a bit confused. Why New Orleans? But it made sense, because that was where the Higgins boats were constructed: the landing craft for D-Day on the Normandy beaches, and every D-Day amphibious assault on the islands of the Pacific.

I visited the museum the first time about a year or two after it opened, when I was in New Orleans for a Budweiser beer convention. I was more interested in the museum than anything happening at the convention.

I visited the museum again in May, 2015, after it was moved and greatly expanded, although the newest wing of the Pacific war, named "The Road to Tokyo," was still in the development stage.

"The Road to Berlin" was fascinating. When a visitor enters the section of the Battle of the Bulge, one truly gets a feel for what it might have like: it is cold, there is snow on the trees and the ground…and it is snowing!

I was so impressed I paid $1,000 to become a member. Maybe because of that several years later I began receiving brochures about WWII Museum tours in the European theater, particularly the D-Day beaches in Normandy, which I had done myself over four days in May, 2014. Having studied a year in France in '67-68, I am fluent in French; moreover I think I have read most every book about D-Day, so I knew what I was looking at.

It was spring of last year, 2017, that I received the WWII Museum brochure for "The Rise and Fall of Hitler's Germany" tour in September in Germany and Poland, led by historian Alexandra Richie. I had read her book, "Warsaw, 1944," without even knowing who she was.

I couldn't get my credit card out fast enough.

I had never been to Berlin, so I flew there three days in advance of the tour. I attended a concert by the Berliner Philharmonic Orchestra the evening of my arrival on a Friday; the first half of music was by a composer with whom I was unfamiliar; the second half was a Bruckner Symphony.

The conductor conducted all the pieces from memory.

Which made me so proud that this past February 4th, I had conducted the Bismarck-Mandan Symphony Orchestra in the Finale to Igor Stravinsky's "Firebird Ballet" from memory.

Except that was only about four minutes. The Berliner Orchestra conductor had memorized hours of compositions.

Just being there in that symphony hall was a once-in-a-lifetime experience. Is there a better symphony venue on Earth? Or a better symphony orchestra?

I flew to Berlin early for two other reasons: to get my bearings on my own (I don't entirely trust tours), and I wanted to visit the Museum of Jewish History, which was not on the tour itinerary, but, maybe should be.

Saturday morning, from my hotel near Potsdammerplatz, I walked the few blocks to the center of Berlin. The first thing I encountered was the monument to the Jewish Holocaust, which consists of concrete blocks covering about a five acre space, no two the same dimension, representing the untold individuals who perished; each had his/her story to tell. But their individual stories are forever lost.

I must admit that I am none too fond of Germans, because I know their history, especially their military history from the time of Bismarck. Also I have had some very nasty personal encounters with ugly Germans while they were touring abroad; Germans just don't seem to travel well.

I agreed with my French wife's farmer uncle, Pierrot, when we were visiting at their house during the reunification of the two Germanies. Pierrot asked me my opinion, and I replied that I was optimistic but skeptical. He replied, in French, "They worry me; they are far too fond of parades."

But I must give credit to the two succeeding generations of Germans, who followed the generation of their fathers and mothers and their grandfathers and grandmothers, who were Nazis or Nazi collaborators: they have done a marvelous job in their monuments and museums to atone – or try -- for what was perpetrated by the generation of WWII.

That was my thought as I left the Holocaust Memorial to view the Brandenburg Gate and stroll Unter den Linden, the famous main street of Berlin. Unter den Linden reminded me of Place Pompidou near the Pompidou Museum of Contemporary Art in Paris, with its performing street artists, its political demonstrators, demonstrating futilely against something or another, and its sidewalk food vendors.

Except in Paris you will NEVER find a food vendor selling stacks of pretzels the size of small pizzas, nor Currywurst.

These are two of the favorite gustatory "delicacies" of the Hun.

I will get to that later.

First, the Berlin Museum of Jewish History.

It occupies two buildings: the entrance is a 19th century baroque building, that includes a restaurant and open interior plaza; the museum itself is in a modern building designed by the Polish

Jewish architect, David Liebeskind, who survived the Holocaust as a child. He also designed the new New York City World Trade Center.

Liebeskind's building, from above, looks like a kind of zig-zag. Inside it is a labyrinth; in many corners one runs into a dead-end, designed to give the visitor a feel for the dead-end of the gas chambers.

The museum, on the top floor, is one of the most fascinating I have ever visited; the history of the Jews from the time of the Babylonian captivity, to the Diaspora throughout Europe, through medieval times, and their increasing economic importance in later centuries, but always the anti-Semitic persecutions and their confinement to ghettos, through the Nazi Holocaust, to this day in modern Germany, which has only a small remnant of the former Jewish population.

An irony itself. Because the Jewish population in Germany during Hitler's time was a small minority. Most of the Jews killed in the Holocaust were from the countries defeated and occupied by the Wehrmacht. In the east: Poland, the Baltics, Byelorussia and Ukraine in the Soviet Union, Slovakia, Hungary, Bulgaria, Romania, the Balkans, and Greece; in the west: Holland, Belgium, and France. Also Italy after the Germans took control.

The tour started that Monday, with the arrival of the participants at the Berlin Regent Hotel and an evening introductory cocktail party and dinner.

I took a taxi to the Regent from my hotel, and, since I had not eaten breakfast, I went outside to find a restaurant, spotting one on a corner only a half-block from the Regent: "La Gendamerie," French for "The Police Station." I thought the name a bit odd. But I was excited at my luck in finding a

French restaurant in the center of Berlin. Except the dishes on the sidewalk menu board were not French but German.

I was about to turn away to continue my search for a restaurant when a waiter stepped out of the door, and said to me, "Sir, you need to try our restaurant, which is the finest in all Berlin."

I am a sucker for a good sales pitch.

I replied, "Well if I have lunch in your restaurant, don't you think I should be the judge of that? What do you suggest?"

He asked if I had tried Currywurst, sliced liver sausage sprinkled with Curry powder, smothered in a sweet catsup and served with what I call "artificial" French Fries: flash-frozen, not fresh. I had seen people eating this on Unter den Linden next to portable food stands; it didn't look very appetizing to me.

He said, "It is the most popular dish in all of Berlin!"

My travel motto has always been, "When in Rome, do as the Romans do."

So I sat on a seat at the bar, the waiter ordered a dish of Currywurst, and I ordered a draught beer from a local brewery.

I am a retired beer distributor, so when I travel I always make a point of observing the local beer scene. In the United States with the advent and subsequent popularity of so-called craft beers, it is common for a tavern or restaurant to offer 40-60 or more different beers. As a distributor we have had to adapt accordingly; when I was active in the business we had, maybe, 50-75 SKUs (individual packages); now we have more than 1,000. Has our volume increased incrementally? Nope. It is simply that the market is more fragmented. And our inventory carrying costs have increased dramatically. Same for the taverns, restaurants, and the package stores we serve.

Not so much in Europe, particularly Germany.

The most draught beer handles I have ever seen in a tavern or restaurant is four: two local lagers, a wheat beer, and a dark beer. Usually it is only two: a lager and a wheat beer. Want a different lager or a dark beer? It will be in a bottle or a can.

When I point out the difference between the US and the European bar/restaurant to the bartender, I always get this response: "Why?"

Good question.

While I waited for my Currywurst the waiter who had invited me in handed me a coffee table style picture book of the modern history of Germany, which began with Chancellor Bismarck in the mid-nineteenth century; it was he who organized the multitude of states, fiefdoms, and duchies into what we now know as Germany.

The publisher was a company called Tauschen, but I didn't think to look for a publishing date, although I later assumed it was mid-to-late 1950s. I assumed this because the last picture of the Third Reich, prior to the September 1, 1939, invasion of Poland was of Hitler in the center of a crowd of Nazi officials whose right arms are outstretched in the "Heil, Hitler!" salute. The next page was a picture of bombed out Berlin in 1945.

Nothing! Absolutely nothing about Germany's waging war in Europe for six plus years. Nothing about the defeat of the Wehrmacht. Or Hitler's suicide in late April, 1945. And, of course, nothing about the Holocaust and the concentration and death camps.

Alexandra Richie, our tour historian, told me when I

mentioned the book that it was common practice for many years to suppress any reminder of what had happened in Germany, and what the Germans had done in Europe in WWII.

I regret now that I didn't try to buy it.

My dish of catsup-smothered Currywurst arrived with a paper container of artificial French Fries. At first I tried a taste of the catsup, which was far too sweet for me. So I scraped it off as best I could from a slice of the white liver sausage encased in an animal intestine. And took a bite.

I immediately pushed the entire mess away from me and drank a deep gulp of the beer.

Whereupon the bartender came running the length of the bar. "What is wrong?"

Me: "This is the most popular dish in all Berlin?"

Bartender: "Berliners just love it."

Me: "No wonder you people lost two world wars! Sending your soldiers to invade innocent countries with shit like this in their guts!"

The bartender didn't take offense. He never even batted an eye. He didn't look very German; I think he was a refugee from the Middle East.

I finished the beer. Which was quite good.

World War II in Berlin

Our tour officially began with the welcome cocktail party and dinner at the Regent Hotel. It was at the cocktail party that I met Alexandra Richie, telling her with pride that I had read her second book twice, "Warsaw, 1944," about the Polish Warsaw uprising, which was brutally put down by German SS units, and her first, "Berlin," a voluminous, well-researched history of the city.

Alexandra was born in Canada, but educated at Oxford, England, where she met her Polish husband; they now reside in Warsaw, where Alexandra teaches history in Polish at the University. Her husband's father, who survived incarceration at the original Auschwitz, provided her the material and inspiration to write her book about the Warsaw uprising.

Dinner was more gourmet than my Currywurst lunch. But it was duck breast, served the European way, meaning nearly raw: a piece of dark red meat oozing blood. I passed. The wine was quite good, as was the chocolate dessert.

You are probably thinking that I only had that chocolate dessert as food the entire day.

But after I finished my beer in "La Gendamerie," I walked a few blocks and discovered the wonderful French department store, "Galleries Lafayette," with a variety of French restaurants in the basement, including a Breton-style creperie; I enjoyed a black wheat gallette with cheese, onions, and ham and a glass of Muscadet, my favorite French white wine.

"When in Rome, do as the Romans do!"

The First Morning

We boarded a bus for a walking tour of central Berlin, first stop: the Memorial to the Holocaust that I had visited my first morning in Berlin.

I was fortunate to spend some quality time alone with Alexandra Richie. I told her that in all my reading about the rise of the Third Reich, Hitler, the war of annihlation waged by the German Wehrmacht and the SS Units, and the Holocaust, I have never been able to reconcile the fact that one of the most learned, cultured,

religious peoples on Earth, the
Germans of that era, were capable
of committing the worst atrocities
against humanity in history.

Many of the worst offenders in the
army, the SS, those in charge of the
concentration camps and the death
camps, so many rank-and file
common citizens involved in the
worst forms of cruelty and murder
were teachers, doctors, lawyers,
judges...the professions. There was
the expected share of riff-raff and
criminals. But from what I have
read, they were mostly in the
lower ranks.

At bottom, were they really just
"The Hun?" Was cruelty in their
national gene, their blood?

Alexandra hesitated before
answering: "I don't really know.
Because I have spent a great deal
of time in Berlin and Germany, and
I have never seen that side of these
people."

"It is very complicated. And one must consider and study the time and circumstances and background of what happened then."

I agreed. I agree now.

The rise of Nazism and Hitler that lead to WWII in Europe and the Holocaust was "The Perfect Storm" of pent-up German nationalism, bitterness over the loss of the Great War, the suffering and humiliation caused by the subsequent Treaty of Versailles, and long-latent anti-Semitism fanned into a fury by Hitler and his minions, who blamed the Jews for "the stab in the back" that forced Germany to surrender in WWI; after all, their armed forces surrendered without having been truly defeated.

Still.

One has to stand in amazement of the horror and the millions of dead caused by Germany's "Perfect Storm."

May it never happen again.

But it could.

A woman on the tour asked Alexandra if what happened to the Jews was common knowledge among the German populace.

I stated I thought it was. I had read at least one book, "Hitler's Willing Executioners," which gave numerous examples of willing collaboration in the Holocaust by many individuals as well as town populaces.

Alexandra disagreed, pointing out what she had written in "Berlin," about the Nazi era, that while many thousands were aware of what was happening to the Jews, because they worked in transportation or archives or other participating departments, the average Frankfort Frau, by way of example, probably was unaware that her Jewish neighbors were being murdered, although she might have wondered why they no longer lived next door.

Perhaps.

Allied interrogation teams and correspondents who followed the conquering armies into western Germany were frustrated to find that individual Germans almost universally declared they had never been Nazis or Nazi sympathizers; many claimed they hated the Nazis.

Famed WWII correspondent, Martha Gellhorn, wrote:

"No one is a Nazi. No one ever was. There may have been some Nazis in the next village, and, as a matter of fact, in the town about twenty kilometers away it was a veritable hotbed of Nazidom…We have done nothing wrong. We were never Nazis!...It would sound better if it were set to music. Then the Germans could sing this refrain.

They all talk like this. One asks oneself how the Nazi government to which no one paid allegiance managed to carry on this war for five and a half years. Obviously not a man, woman or child in Germany ever approved of the war."

Maybe the truth lies somewhere between Alexandra's opinion and mine: many, many Germans knew about the atrocities and how the war was being waged; most could not bring themselves to admit it. Or refused.

Our Tour of WWII Berlin

I will just summarize some highlights.

The Museum of Terror.

Housed in the former Gestapo Headquarters, where thousands of "enemies of the Third Reich:" read: anyone in opposition, from communists to the Catholic clergy, and Jews, were tortured and murdered.

Potsdam.

Where the final summit of the Allies was held following the German Unconditional Surrender in early May, 1945. The first meetings included Stalin, Truman, and Churchill. But Churchill lost the election as Prime Minister, much to his chagrin, and was replaced by Clement Atlee.

One of the only agreements that came out of this conference was the demand that Japan surrender unconditionally. But Stalin wanted some of the spoils if, as happened, Russian invaded Manchuria. Stalin never got what he wanted because Truman came away not trusting him.

Churchill had originally wanted Stalin to concede Poland and other territories in Eastern Europe, but he was voted out of office, and Stalin's Russian armies occupied all of Eastern Europe, including much of Germany, and he wasn't about to give up an inch of it.

Thus began the Cold War.

The Museum of the Berlin Airlift.

In 1948, when Stalin had the three overland routes from Western Germany blocked into West Berlin, the United States, Britain, France, Canada, and Australia mounted a gigantic, round-the-clock airlift to keep West Berlin provisioned, especially with coal to heat the houses and buildings during a bitter winter.

After eleven months more supplies were being airlifted than were delivered overland before the blockade; Stalin relented. It was the first confrontation of the Cold War.

The Berlin Wall.

Construction of the wall began in 1961, to stop the flight of East German citizens for a better life in West Germany; some 3.5 million people had already made the crossing. After the wall was completed, it averaged approximately 13 feet in height, was 97 miles long; it completely surrounded West Berlin, with guard towers and a strip known as "No Man's Land." Following its completion the number of escapes dwindled to practically zero.

There are countless heartbreaking stories about how the wall separated families and relatives from one another during its existence. And some 200 individuals died trying to breach it.

The wall was opened in 1989, and demolition was completed in 1992.

Today there exist only remnants as reminders of what once was. We visited a section that contained the original wall, the strip of "No Man's Land," and an East German guard tower. What I wanted to see, but was told we didn't have time, was the section containing original graffiti by West German street artists, one in particular of Russian President Leonid Brezhnev in a lip lock with East German President, Eric Honnekker.

The Reichstag.

This building is the equivalent of our capital building in Washington, DC; construction began in 1894; it was gutted by fire 27 February, 1933, not even one month after Hitler became Chancellor. To this day no one knows how the fire got started, but the Communists were blamed, which resulted in the Nazis getting the "Enabling Act" passed, which granted Hitler dictatorial power.

Even though the Reichstag was never used between 1933 and the Russian conquest of Berlin in April and May, 1945, nevertheless General's Zukhov's troops took it as the symbol of the Third Reich, units scrambling in dangerous fighting for the right to place the hammer and sickle flag of the Soviet Union on top of the building.

In the early 1990s an architectural contest was waged, won by the British architect, Norman Foster, to restore and modernize the Reichstag, which we visited, enjoying a rather nice non-Teutonic lunch in the restaurant. Norman Foster left the stone outer walls intact, including Russian graffiti, virtually inserting a modern building inside, complete with a high dome, from which one can have a panoramic view of Berlin. The Reichstag is once again the home of unified Germany's Parliament.

Hitler's Bunker.

It is now a parking lot. The bunker itself was filled in for good reason: to prevent any veneration of Hitler and the Nazis by todays neo-Nazis.

The Wanssee Conference.

To me this just has to be the most despicable single meeting in the history of mankind on Earth.

It occurred January 20, 1942, in a villa on the shores of Lake Wanssee, outside Berlin, called by the evil Reinhard Heydrich, under secret oral orders from Hitler through Heinrich Himmler, to determine "The Final Solution to the Jewish Question." In other words: the mass murder of the eleven million Jews, men, women, and children in the German occupied countries of Europe. Fifteen men were present, representing various "interested" Third Reich government departments; Adolf Eichman took the minutes.

Maybe there is something to be said about the innate cruelty of the Hun. The Wanssee Conference is proof that such is not a generalization. At least not about the Nazis in control of Germany of that time.

All fifteen participants were in full agreement that eleven million individuals should die simply because they were who they were: Jews.

By war's end they had nearly succeeded.

Dresden

We departed Berlin by bus to drive to the city of Dresden, famous or infamous because it was a beautiful medieval city, of no strategic value to the Allies, full of refugees from all over Europe and many American POWs from the Battle of the Bulge, but nevertheless destroyed by first a night attack with incendiary bombs dropped by British Bomber Command, which ignited a conflagration, followed the next day by a daylight raid with incendiary bombs by the American Eighth Air Force.

So why was it attacked and destroyed? Most historians point to the head of British Bomber command, known as "Bomber Harris," whose personal mission was to destroy all German cities. Dresden hadn't been bombed; so it needed to be bombed, he reasoned. And the Americans went along.

Kurt Vonnegut, a POW from the Battle of the Bulge, worked as a slave laborer in a pork slaughter house in Dresden; he describes the ordeal Dresden suffered in his book, "Slaughterhouse 5."

We must have arrived late for our guided tour of Dresden, as our local guide fairly sprinted through the tour; most of us could not keep up.
And he didn't like questions. Especially one from me: "If the buildings we are seeing are restored, why are all the facades black with soot?"

But I needn't have asked the question, as I knew the answer. Dresden for years was in East Germany, which was one of the most polluted countries in all of

Europe, along with the countries of the former "Soviet Block."

Trucks spewed uncontrolled, black clouds of diesel fumes. And the few cars that existed were Trabants, of East German fabrication, with two-cycle engines that spread a swath of stinky pollution wherever they passed.

My first encounter with a Trabant had occurred some fifteen years prior in Slovakia, when my wife and I, driving a new German rental car, overtook one on a narrow two-lane road on a hill. It was impossible to pass. So we had to sit behind the slow-moving Trabant while it spewed forth a noxious cloud of black smoke. Finally, I pulled over for a number of minutes to clear the air in our car.

When I told the proprietor of the hotel in Zakopane, Poland, about our experience, he just laughed, explaining that the Trabant was the East German poor cousin of the West German Volkswagen. In East

Germany, if you desired, and could afford a car, the Trabant was it.

He said the Trabant could be ordered with only one option, which was absolutely necessary: a heated rear window.

I said, "A heated rear window?"

"To keep your hands warm while you pushed it to the nearest garage."

Wroclaw-Krakow-Auschwitz

We overnighted in Wroclaw, Poland, formerly Breslau, Germany, staying in what we all thought was the weirdest hotel ever, followed by a guided tour the next morning, which I found less than interesting.

After an afternoon drive we arrived at a hotel in Krakow, Poland.

My wife and I had spent a day and night in Krakow some fifteen years earlier, after three nights in Budapest, Hungary, and a night in Zakopane, Poland.

The main square of Krakow was only a few blocks from our hotel, so we walked all over the historic town, stopping in one of the numerous outdoor cafes for lunch and to people watch.

About mid-afternoon Maryvonne said she was tired and wanted to return to the hotel for a nap. I told her I would scope out a restaurant for that evening, preferably one that didn't serve the usual Eastern European fare that had us in a constant state of bloat.

Finding none, I gave up, and on my walk back to the hotel, went into a bar to sample a glass of Polish vodka. The waiter spoke English. After a taste, I asked him the name of the vodka, and he said, "Belvedere," a top-shelf brand.

I said, "Belvedere? I can get that in most any bar in Bismarck, North

Dakota. Don't you have some real Polish vodka?"

Whereupon he produced a glass of amber liquid with a blade of grass. I took a sip, pronounced it excellent, with a smooth, rounded texture.

"What is this?"

"Buffalo Grass vodka, made from potatoes, and flavored with the grass eaten by Polish wild buffalo."

Of all things, as we left the hotel that evening to try to find a restaurant with edible food, what should we stumble upon? A French restaurant that served some of the best French dishes we have ever enjoyed! Maryvonne had a fresh filet of fish from the Baltic Sea, to the north of Poland, and I had sautéed duck liver, washed down with a wonderful Beaujolais red wine.

Our WWII group was on its own for dinner. I didn't find the same

French restaurant as before, but I did find a different one on the same street just off the main square. I had spaghetti with fresh mussels and a carafe of dry, white wine. Perfect.

The next morning was a retracing of the movie, "Schindler's List."

Sort of.

There is little left to see.

We went to Oskar Schindler's former enamel factory, in which he employed "his" Jews. But it is now occupied by a new factory, and we weren't allowed in.

We walked around the grounds of the former "Plaszow" Concentration Camp, but there is now only a large monument.

The main square was the only thing somewhat recognizable as the gathering place for the Jews before they were loaded into the cattle cars for transport to

Auschwitz, from which they were rescued by Schindler.

They were the lucky ones.

The next day we had a three-hour guided tour of Auschwitz I and the death factory of Birkenau.

Three hours.

Contrast that with the six hour tour Maryvonne and I had some fifteen years earlier. It was on a Sunday in September, during that heat wave in Europe that killed so many elderly who lacked air conditioning. And the air conditioning in our new rental car that we had driven from Vienna wasn't working.

After breakfast we left our hotel in Krakow for the one hour drive to Auschwitz on a winding, two lane asphalt road, through dense forest interspersed with fields of small grain crops.

By the time we arrived in Auschwitz for our tour the temperature was approaching 100 degrees Fahrenheit. It reminded me about what I had read regarding the Jews from Greece, who arrived in similar heat. Most were already dead, having gone days without food and water; their bodies had to be unloaded off the cattle cars to be incinerated.

If you want to visit Auschwitz you are required to be on a tour, led by an authorized guide. Our tour group was ten or so Americans. Our tour guide was a Polish woman in her forties, born and raised in the nearby town of Oswiecim, the Polish name for Auschwitz, pronounced "Osh-wee-i-sheem." "Auschwitz" is the German name.

We began at Auschwitz I, with its infamous entrance gate over which is the iconic curved wrought iron sign with the words, "Arbeit Mach Frei," "Work makes you free."

Except nearly every person who walked through this gate, no matter how hard he worked, died. Either from work on a starvation diet or in the torture chambers.

Auschwitz I is a collection of reddish brick barracks buildings constructed for the former Polish army, located just east of the German border in Poland at a key intersection of multiple rail lines.

At first it was intended as a work camp for Polish prisoners: Catholic clergy, the intelligentsia, government officials and the nobility. In addition to the Jews, Gypsies, homosexuals, and anyone else they didn't like, the Germans were determined to enslave then annihilate all the Poles as part of their plan of "Lebensraum," freeing up the lands of the East to be settled by German farmers.

When Germany invaded Poland on September 1, 1939, and later the Soviet Union on June 22, 1941, its armies were followed by

"Einsatzgruppen," "Special Action Teams," that were charged with killing Jews and other enemies of the Reich. The methods they used were up front and personal: they simply lined up their victims next to deep ditches the victims themselves were forced to dig and shot them in the back of the head. This was the method that killed the majority of the Jews of Eastern Europe; in fact, the majority of all Jews killed during the war.

It was after the Wannsee Conference in January, 1942, that a "cleaner" way of mass murder was called for, not only to spare German soldiers the stress of shooting men, women, and children, but to speed up the process of killing the estimated 11-12 million Jews in Europe.

Thus the extermination camps were constructed: among others Treblinka, Sobibor, Chelmo, and Auschwitz-Birkinau, which became synonymous with death on a mass scale.

The start of our tour began in the main floor hallway of one of the numerous barracks buildings; the hallway was lined with pictures and name of the Polish men who were the first victims. The Germans, with their obsession for accurate records had, at first, been that meticulous. As the killings increased they no longer kept records, except for the number of transports received and "processed."

Those pictures were haunting; they were the "before" Auschwitz I pictures, taken as the prisoners were registered in the camp. But they were already emaciated, close to skeletal. Their future life could be calculated in mere weeks, given a daily allowance of 700 calories, accompanied by a brutal dawn to dusk work schedule of manual labor, beatings, and for many, torture.

Daily morning and evening roll calls involved public hangings of prisoners for the slightest offense by way of "example."

One of the barracks buildings was used solely for torture. In addition to the rooms in which tools were used to crush skulls and extract fingernails, the lower level contained the "stand-up" torture rooms into which prisoners were crammed with no food or water until they died…standing up.
Our Polish guide told our group that she had two uncles who were in Auschwitz. One died in a "stand up" torture room. The other uncle survived. She said when she was young she couldn't understand why he always had a piece of bread he carried in a pocket. She asked her mother about it, who said she would explain it all when she was older.

I had read that Auschwitz has three million visitors per year. I asked our Polish guide how many of them were German. She replied, "Almost no-one from that time, only occasional student groups."

She then told us she absolutely detested Germans, not only for what they did to the Jews and Gypsies and so many others, but because they wanted to kill the Poles for their land. She said that she normally worked in the archives to help families identify relatives who perished there, but that she was called to escort us Americans. She said she would never take a German group on a tour.

In Auschwitz I we saw entire rooms, behind glass, filled to the ceilings with suitcases, eye glasses, baby shoes, and human hair. One exhibit displayed how the Nazis used the hair of victims to make blankets for their U-boat submariners. The blankets still reek of Zyklon-B, the gas used to asphyxiate victims in the gas chambers.

Our guide paused before each exhibit to emphasize, "This is one more proof that the Holocaust happened, and happened on a monstrous scale here.

After several of her reminders, I pulled her aside to explain that I was a student of WWII and the Holocaust, that she was "...preaching to the choir."

Her response shocked me.

She said, "Sam, you wouldn't believe how many people come through here, do the tour, and still cannot comprehend what happened here. A few of them are Holocaust deniers, that none of this took place; whenever I have such a person or persons on one of my tours, I summarily get them kicked off the premises. Who can deny what they are seeing?"

We then left Auschwitz I, and boarded a bus for Birkenau, the labor and death camp that was the personal project of Heinrich Himmler, whom Hitler put in charge of the Holocaust.

Auschwitz I can be called a happenstance: the barracks buildings were already built near the junction of several convenient railroads, so it was first used as a work camp, although the first gas chamber and crematorium were built on the grounds to begin experimentation with poisonous gasses; the first victims of Zyklon-B were Soviet POWs.

Birkenau was prima facie created to be a work/death factory. Its most iconic feature is its tall wooden guard structure, beneath which two enormous doors swung open to receive the train transports of those condemned to die simply because of who they were.

We followed our guide through those open doors to the rail siding where the transports were emptied out for the "selektion" to decide who was able-bodied enough to work before being gassed and those who were to be gassed immediately.

Our guide said this was the very spot where Doctor Joseph Mengele would greet nearly every transport to identify identical twins and wrench them away from their parents for his horrific experiments on them in the name of scientific research, but which was nothing more than sadistic quackery.

We have identical twin granddaughters. They are beautiful, intelligent, charming, and gifted athletes. I already knew much about Mengele. But when our guide brought this up it was like a sucker punch to the gut. Maryvonne turned pale, began to wretch, and told me she did not want to continue the tour; she had seen enough.

We did complete the tour of Birkenau, including a barracks building into which emaciated prisoners were crowded in lice-infested bunkbeds. Also a latrine building, which contained a long raised concrete platform lined with two rows of holes, one on each side, in which inmates were allowed to relieve themselves in the morning before roll call without the benefit of anything with which to wipe themselves; why paper currency was so valuable; as currency it was worthless but it was invaluable to wipe oneself.

The crematoria are still there, but in ruins. The Nazis blew them up in an effort to destroy the evidence of Auschwitz before the Soviet Army arrived. Adult prisoners were evacuated on a forced march back to Germany. Few survived. The Soviets found some children who were awaiting death in the gas chambers; the Nazis had tattooed their left forearms for identification.

Back in the visitor center we guzzled bottled water to rehydrate from the heat. Our guide asked if anyone had any last questions.

Among our group of ten or so Americans was a middle-aged couple from New Jersey; the woman said she had a question: "Do you mean to tell me that people actually died here?"

Without so much as an acknowledgement of this woman's question, our guide turned to me and said, "See what I mean?"

Gdansk

Most Americans know it as Danzig, the port city in the north of Poland on the Baltic Sea, the home to the Polish Solidarity movement, led by dock-worker Lech Walesa, that resulted in the overthrow of the communist government, which had ruled Poland with an iron fist since the end of WWII in 1945.

But what most people don't know is that Gdansk was one of the first battlegrounds when the Germans launched their attack September 1, 1939.

The excuse for launching this unprovoked attack was staged. German concentration camp inmates, wearing Polish army uniforms, attacked a German radio station on the German-Poland border, killing other concentration camp inmates wearing German army uniforms.

The "retaliatory, vengeance" attack was on.

All of the concentration camp inmates who took part in this charade were murdered.

A German warship just happened to be in the port of Gdansk, on a "good-will" mission, when the attack began farther to the southwest; it opened fire, starting the battle for Gdansk.

Gdansk WWII Museum

Except for the section, "The Road to Berlin," in the WWII Museum in New Orleans this is the best museum of the war in Europe I

have ever visited. It begins with
propaganda posters from the rise
of Fascism and Benito Mussolini in
Italy and the rise of the Nazis in
Germany, including depictions of
male Jews with exaggerated long
noses and sinister looks. It ends
with a railroad cattle car used to
transport Jews to the death camps,
and a haunting section of
thousands of pictures of Jews who
were murdered.

We were allowed two hours to
visit on our own. We could have
stayed all day.

The Wolfsschanze

Hitler, Goering, and Himmler, in
spite of their inhuman cruelty,
have always struck me as comical
characters; they were like little
boys playing with toy soldiers,
waging war on a board. All three of
them, but Goering and Himmler in
particular, had an obsession with
uniforms, constantly designing
new ones. Goering had a
pronounced fetish for medals, with

which he always bedecked his latest uniform creation.

So also the names they gave the battle headquarters: The "Adler Horst," "Eagles Nest," in the West; and "The Wolfsschanz," "The Wolf's Den," in the East (Pomerania).

If you want to get a feel for The Wolfsschanze, a good start is to watch the movie, "Valkyrie," starring Tom Cruise, as Count Claus Stauffenberg, about the July 20, 1944, assassination attempt on Hitler in a war planning building on the grounds of The Wofsschanze. Stauffenburg planted a bomb in a briefcase, which he placed under the table next to Hitler. But after he left the building the briefcase was moved; when the bomb went off Hitler was shaken up, his ear-drums pierced, but he was not killed. Subsequently, in a paroxysm of revenge, he had Stauffenburg and his co-conspirators shot or hanged, along with many hundreds more suspected of being complicit or knowing about the plot.

There is no longer much to see of the Wolfsschanze, the many concrete bunker buildings mostly destroyed by the Soviet Army that overran the fortifications. Hitler's assassination bunker has pancaked upon itself. The only intact bunker is that of Martin Borman, Hitler's personal secretary, which, is a blackened cement hulk one can only see from the outside.

The large map of The Wolfsschanze shows that each of the Third Reich higher ups required his own personal bunker: Hitler, Goering, Goebbels, Himmler, Borman, Albert Speer, and Generals Jodl and Keitel.

Little boys playing at real war.

Warsaw

The last stop on our WWII tour.

I expected to find a completely rebuilt, modern city.

Because Hitler ordered Himmler to completely destroy Warsaw when the Poles staged their uprising in August, 1944. It is all described in Alexandra Richie's book, "Warsaw, 1944."

I had read it a couple of years before this tour; it made sick to my stomach then. Prior to the tour I read it a second time, but I almost didn't finish it.
Himmler had called in several of the most notorious of the Einsatzgruppen, the "Special Action" troops charged with shooting Jews, Russian partisans, and Russian commissars on the Eastern Front.

The murder, rapes, and destruction they committed were unprecedented in warfare of any era.

Most of Warsaw is a rebuilt city with modern buildings.

But I was surprised, and most pleased to learn, that the Bristol Hotel, where we spent our last nights, the adjacent main government building, and the central part of Warsaw had been rebuilt to nearly what it looked like in the 18th century, based on cityscapes painted by the Italian, Cannelletto.

Warsaw defiance in the face of Hitler's order to raze Warsaw from the face of the Earth.
And good for the citizens of Warsaw and Poland. May it never happen again.

The tragedy was that Warsaw, between WW I and the German invasion of September 1, 1939, had become a prosperous, vibrant, cultured capital, known as the "Paris of Poland." The Nazi invasion ended all that.

Our tour group stopped at the former train platform where the Jews of the Warsaw ghetto were loaded into cattle cars, 2,000 or more at a time, for the short trip to the extermination center of Treblinka.

But there is little to see now; just a plaque.

We also wandered the Jewish cemetery. But I am not sure why. Maybe to give us a sense that before the Nazi invasion, life…and death…was normal for the Jews.

There are no Jews buried therein who perished in the Holocaust.

Later that evening we were bused to the Museum of the Polish Warsaw Uprising in August-September, 1944, the subject of Alexandra Richie's second book.

I found the museum fascinating, but our time to visit was limited, as the supposed highlight of our Warsaw visit was an evening spent with four of the still living Polish participants in the Uprising, now in their 90s.

Normally, I would have found this a fascinating experience. And, no doubt it was for those who understood Polish, or those seated in the nearby tables, who were close to the translator.

Unfortunately our table was at the far end of a large room from which a WWII American bomber was suspended from the ceiling; the acoustics were horrible, consequently we heard nothing. Thank goodness the wine was good and plentiful.

The next day we were given a guided tour of the Museum of the History of the Jews in Poland, the finest, most complete history of the Jews I have visited, even better than the one in Berlin

Our tour ended with a catered dinner at the summer retreat in the countryside outside of Warsaw owned by Alexandra Richie and her husband, who, unfortunately we never met.

Alexandra apologized in advance for the modest place where we would finish our tour.

She needn't have. It was fabulous.

A country estate one might have had in Poland before September 1, 1939.

REFIGHTING WWII IN THE PACIFIC

"Victory in the Pacific" Tour with the WWII Museum, March, 2018

Background

When I first visited the original WWII Museum in New Orleans, it was almost entirely about the D-Day landings in Normandy, France, June 6, 1944. Probably because that was of most interest to historian/founder, Stephen Ambrose.

However there was a small section devoted to the war in the Pacific theater, in which my father participated as a Marine. Dad had two tours in the Pacific during the war.

The first was on Guadalcanal, but he landed after the Marines had mopped up the Japanese, so he really didn't see much, if any fighting. He was in charge of teams that packed parachutes for the F4-U Corsair, the famous gull-winged fighter-bomber. Dad claimed he packed parachutes for Pappy Boyington's Black Sheep Squadron. I hope he did, because that is a cool story, but I have never been able to corroborate Dad's claim.

He did tell me something that is definitely true.

While Dad was doing his stint on Guadalcanal, the F4-U, manufactured by the Chance-Vought company, a new plane, with associated glitches that needed to be solved, experienced several inadvertent life raft inflations while in flight. Since the life raft was located behind the pilot's seat, the inflated raft pushed the seat and the pilot into the control stick and the instrument panel, resulting in several deaths, plus the loss of the aircraft.

Dad suggested that a bayonet be fixed to the seat to puncture the life raft should it inadvertently inflate. After a bunch of Marine Corps red tape, Dad's idea was adopted. He got a letter of commendation for his "ingenuity" from Admiral Raymond Spruance (famous, beginning with the Battle of Midway), and a promotion to Master Technical Sergeant, which, I was told at his funeral in 1992, was nearly an impossible promotion in rank for an enlisted man, even during WWII.

While I was in the small Pacific theater section of the original WWII Museum, which mostly consisted of US anti-Japanese posters: short, black-haired men with crossed eyes, buck teeth, and thick, black-rimmed glasses, referred to in the posters as "Japs, Nips, and Yellowbellied Slants (this was way before "Political Correctness"), I found myself staring at a photo of the Essex Class aircraft carrier, Bunker Hill, billowing huge clouds of black smoke after two Kamikaze hits.

There was a rather short man next to me, whom I guessed to be my father's age, at the time, looking at the same picture.

I asked him, "Are you looking at the picture of Bunker Hill?"

"Yes. Why?"

"My father was on that carrier when it was attacked."

He turned, staring at me for several seconds, and said, "You are very lucky to be alive."

He told me that his ship was leaving Bremerton Harbor, west of Seattle, Washington, when Bunker Hill sailed past under its own power. He said that almost everyone left his battle station to see Bunker Hill. No one could believe it was moving under its own power, as it was a completely burned out hulk.

That was sometime in June, 1945.

In late 1945, Bunker Hill was back in the Pacific...not as an operational carrier, but as a troop transport to bring home American POWs.

We could do things like that in WWII.

Not so much anymore.

Bunker Hill

Dad's second stint in the Pacific war was on Bunker Hill.

Read "Japan, 1941," which describes all the turmoil between the Japan militarists and those in government and the diplomats who cautioned against war, which they thought, rightfully so, was unwinnable, because Japan had virtually no natural resources. The militarists won out, and Japan attacked Pearl Harbor on December 7, 1941.

When informed that the Japanese forces had completely surprised the Americans at Pearl Harbor, December 7, 1941, which President Franklin D. Roosevelt, in his address to Congress the following day called, "A date which will live in infamy," Admiral Yamamoto, the architect of the attack on Pearl Harbor, who had studied and lived in the United States, said, "I fear that all we have done is awaken a sleeping giant, and fill him with a terrible resolve."

During the Battle of Midway, six months after Pearl Harbor, the Japanese lost four of its most important aircraft carriers; the US lost one. Japan never replaced those capital ships. Within months we had twenty-four Essex Class carriers under construction of newer, bigger, faster design.

I have Dad's diary.

As Bunker Hill sailed under Golden Gate Bridge in early 1945, after Dad and Mom had married January 10, in St. Mary's Church, at the entrance to San Francisco's Chinatown, he wrote, "I have a lump in my throat."

Bunker Hill proceeded to participate in almost every Pacific theater engagement prior to Okinawa: Rabaul, the Gilberts, Marshalls, Kwajalein, and Eniwetok, Tokyo, Truk, the China coast, the Ryukus, the Bonins, and Iwo Jima.

During those engagements Bunker Hill's F4-U pilots sank or damaged more than one million tons of Japanese shipping and shot down 475 aircraft.

During the attack on Okinawa, prior to the Kamikaze attack, Bunker Hill planes had splashed sixty-seven Jap planes, and the ship herself accounted for fourteen more from its anti-aircraft fire.

Dad was again in charge of parachute packing teams.

Kamikazes attacked on the morning of May 11, 1945. After some 58 days of constant combat, Bunker Hill's crew was not at Battle Quarters; no one expected what was about to happen.

The first Kamikaze, with a 550 lb. bomb attached, hit the flight deck among thirty-four armed, and fueled F4-Us, awaiting takeoff.

The following is a description, written by Correspondent Phelps Adams, who witnessed the destruction on Bunker Hill from another ship, probably the battleship USS Missouri:

"Some of the pilots were blown overboard...but before a move could be made to fight the flames another kamikaze came whining out of the clouds, straight into the deadly anti-aircraft guns of the ship. This plane was a Jap dive bomber – a Judy... riddled with shells...but still he came...he dropped his bomb...in the middle of the blazing planes...then he flipped over."

This second Kamikaze also struck the Bunker Hill's island, the command structure.

The ship began to list. But its engines were still capable of full steam.

It turned into the wind, running at maximum throttle to keep the black clouds of smoke billowing aft.

Then the Captain called for a 70 degree turn to rid the ship of water it had taken on from destroyers and a cruiser to combat the fires. The maneuver worked, and Bunker Hill was saved.

But at a cost of some 395 dead and missing of 600 total casualties out of a complement of 3,400 personnel.

Dad told me reluctantly, when I asked him what was the worst thing he witnessed in WWII: "Watching Marines and Navy sailors stripping watches and jewelry off our dead buddies on the decks of Bunker Hill."

I cannot tell you how many times Dad's reply has nearly gotten me into fist fights in bars with WWII Vets, who claim that no such thing could ever have happened.

But for once, Dad wasn't exaggerating.

What he told me is confirmed in the official history of Bunker Hill, "Danger's Hour," by Maxwell Taylor Kennedy.

Kennedy also relates that during the firefighting on Bunker Hill, one enterprising Navy sailor or Marine donned a gas mask, and descended to the deck containing the post office, where a crewmember of the ship had stashed his earnings from a poker game several nights previously. With an acetylene torch he cut out the post office box and pocketed the proceeds.

During WWII America had sixteen million plus men and women in uniform.

They were not all "La crème de la crème" of US society.

The great irony, according to Maxwell Taylor Kennedy's history, was that Bunker Hill, one of the most powerful ships of its era, conceived solely to battle the Japanese, and help win the war in the Pacific, was sold for scrap in 1989, and...towed to Japan.

Victory in the Pacific Tour: What We Saw and Experienced

The DPAA

The day after the arrival in Hawaii of our tour group of some 140, including ten veterans of WWII, two survivors of Iwo Jima, including Woody Wilson, the last surviving Medal of Honor winner, of some 27 Medal of Honor winners from the battle, we were bused to a complex of modern buildings on Hickam Field: The Defense Prisoner of War/Missing in Action Accounting Agency (DPAA).

I never knew, nor did most of us, that this facility even existed.

It is a gigantic forensic lab, the only one that exists in the world, dedicated to the mission that no American soldier will be left behind: remains are recovered, identified, and whenever possible, repatriated to the family of the fallen soldier.

We saw entire rooms with tables covered with bones and objects associated with the exhumed remains.

We learned that the main purpose of the facility is to identify the remains of WWII, Korean War, and Vietnam Veterans, but that it has also identified the remains of

WWI, Civil War, and Revolutionary War combatants. Also Japanese combatants in WWII, particularly Iwo Jima.

A young, female doctor, told us that she is in charge of a forensic team attempting to identify the remains of some 900 Marines killed in the assault on the atoll of Tarawa in 1943, who were interred in a mass grave, but subsequently exhumed and reinterred individually in the cemetery called "Punch Bowl" on Oahu. We saw the chart with pictures on a hallway wall that her team was on its way to identifying most of the men.

But not all.

The mission of the DPAA is difficult, sometimes impossible, and, therefore, frustrating.

Advances in DNA identification have helped,

But we learned that it is only since 1993 that members of the US armed forces, when inducted, have saliva swabs to identify their DNA in case of death.

DNA testing, when possible, is performed by taking DNA from long bones, preferably an upper arm of a corpse; the results are entered into an extensive data base to attempt to determine a family connection.

The success rate of the DPAA in identifying remains is remarkable.

But the four doctors who participated in our tour told us their greatest frustration was in not being able to identify all the lost soldiers whose remains were in their possession.

I swabbed tears from my eyes leaving this wonderful facility and its great work.

My thought: that it never again be necessary.

USS Missouri

Commissioned in June, 1944, rather late in the war in the Pacific, when battleships were already considered obsolete versus the Essex Class Fast Aircraft Carriers, she participated in the Battle of Okinawa, as did Dad's Bunker Hill.

Although the four Iowa Class battleships, including Missouri, were considered obsolete, and consequently mothballed after the war, two, Iowa and Missouri, were resurrected for Operation Desert Storm against Iraq in 1990. They packed a tremendous amount of firepower. The nine 16 inch cannons on three turrets could lob 3,000 lb. shells 25 miles with an on-target accuracy of 50 yards: close enough for a 3,000 lb. shell.

Missouri is best remembered as the ship that hosted the Japanese surrender on September 2, 1945, presided over by General Douglas Macarthur, who ended the ceremony, after a conciliatory gesture to the Japanese, with 'These proceeding are now concluded."

Thus ended World War II.

USS Arizona

The tremendous explosion that sank Battleship Arizona, during the unprovoked Japanese attack on Pearl Harbor, December 7, 1941, was the beginning of America's involvement in World War II.

The hull of Arizona, which is the coffin of more than nine hundred crew killed during the attack, is a famous monument that is reached by launch from the Pearl Harbor Museum.

At the entrance to the movie theater, where one watches a movie about the attack before boarding the launch, a tough looking, tough talking former Marine told our crowd that the families of survivors of the explosion on Arizona, have the right to have their deceased loved ones interred in Arizona's hull to rejoin their fellow crew members; to date more than forty families have done so.

Visiting the Arizona Memorial is solemn and sobering. Even after 76 years, oil still seeps from the hull; it is said that Arizona weeps for her dead.

Saipan

Our WWII group visited the Marianas islands in the same order as the Marines' assaulted them in WWII; first Saipan, then Tinian, then Guam. The reason for attacking and capturing the northern Marianas was to set them up as forward bases for the new B-29 bomber which was designed for attacking Japanese cities, first from high altitudes, then lower with incendiary bombs that ravaged entire neighborhoods of homes built of wood and paper.

The Marine assault on Saipan in June, 1944, was only supposed to take a few days, but it turned into more than a month-long slog, complete with a Banzai charge as the Marines pressed from the invasion beaches in the south up the island to the north, to Marpi Point, where the official estimate is that 5,000 Japanese civilians committed suicide by jumping off the cliffs.

One of our WWII Museum tour historians stated that it may have been closer to twenty thousand Japanese civilians, pointing out that the Japanese population on Saipan before the assault was 30,000; after the assault: 10,000.

Why did so many die? Why did they, individuals and entire families commit suicide en masse?

Because they believed Japanese military propaganda that US Marines were the meanest motor scooters and baddest go-getters on Earth; that, in order to join the

Corps, one had to kill one's own mother.

And that they were intent on maiming, raping, and killing all the Japanese on Saipan...and eating their children!

I am sure that would have been news, or at least a surprise, to my father, who was a Marine in the Pacific, but especially his mother, who lived into her eighties.

Saipan is shaped like Godzilla, with a high ridge down the middle.

It reminded me of much of Mexico: new luxury resorts across the street from abandoned shopping malls; buildings started, but not finished; sleazy strip malls with the inevitable "Poker Palace," a one room joint in which an islander can lose a month's salary.

On our tour of Saipan we had as our guide a vivacious and eloquent Chomorro (native of the Marianas), who informed us that

Chomorros had lived on Saipan for at least 4,000 years.

She explained that it was "mere chance" that Ferdinand Magellan "discovered" Saipan and the Marianas on his truncated circumnavigation of the globe (because he was killed by natives of another island shortly thereafter).

She rightly pointed out that Ferdinand hadn't "discovered" anything; Saipan and the Marianas had been inhabited for millennia. First by Chomorros, then joined by Spaniards, Germans, and, at the turn of the twentieth century, Japanese immigrants, mostly from Okinawa, escaping overcrowding for free land.

When I remarked to her that this WWII tour was completely different than the Rise and Fall of Hitler's Germany Tour that I had done the previous September, complete with multiple visits to wonderful museums (see previous chapter), she said something I will never forget, "Sam, on this tour in the Pacific, EVERYTHING you see is a museum."

She was right.

What we saw on this "Victory in the Pacific" tour was not so much museums as battle sites: invasion beaches, the locations of banzai charges by desperate Japanese soldiers, entrenched bunkers from which Japanese soldiers could only be extricated by grenades and flamethrowers, cliffs from which Japanese civilians threw themselves and their families to their deaths to avoid perceived atrocities by US Marines.

We saw only a very few rusted guns and tanks on this entire trip. It required knowledge of the battles and a bit of imagination to comprehend what the combatants on both sides must have endured.

Tinian

We flew the short hop from Saipan to the airport near Tinian Town in old piston, twin-engine Piper Navajos that had a maximum carrying capacity of eight passengers plus pilot and co-pilot...depending on total weight. So each of us had to be weighed while holding onto whatever we were bringing on board for our day trip. James, our WWII Museum historian, announced in a loud voice that he would only accept bills in large denominations to keep from shouting out any given person's total weight.

Our first stop was a monument to the Seabees, the construction personnel who followed up a successful island capture to build operational bases; in the case of Tinian, the largest, busiest airport in the world at the time, from which, during a bomber launch on Japan, a B-29 took off every 52 seconds.

When shown a map of Tinian, the Seabees commander said it reminded him of the shape of lower Manhattan; he was from Manhattan, so he remade Tinian into "Manhattan in the Pacific," complete with streets named "Broadway" and "Fifth Avenue," and a recreational and hospital area called "Central Park."

Although it took assaulting marines only about a week to "secure" Tinian after Saipan, the Seabees were harassed by remnants of Japanese units; it required months to make Tinian ready to receive B-29s. Eventually the entire island was remade into an air base, with four airfields, hard pads to park B-29s, ordinance storage buildings, barracks, control facilities, and a recreational hall, etc., all supplied by ships anchored in the harbor of Tinian Town on the southwestern part of the island.

The two most important runways, "Able" and "Bravo," were located on an East-West axis on the north end of Tinian, named "North Field." Nearby are two large pits, "A" and "B," designed to load atomic bombs, which were too large and heavy to be loaded conventionally. Only "B" was used to load "Little Boy" (a uranium device) into the B-29 named "Enola Gay," dropped on Hiroshima August 6, 1945, and "Fat Man" (a more powerful plutonium bomb) into Bock's Car, dropped on Nagasaki on August 9. Both planes took off from Runway Able.

In truth there is not much to see on Tinian anymore. The one-time "World's Busiest Airport" is quiet now, overgrown by choking vegetation. Again, a visit requires use of one's knowledge of the history of the place, and a bit of imagination.

We never got a satisfactory explanation of an array of some half-dozen, very tall radio towers on the west side of the island, other than that they belonged to "Voice of America."

What?

VOA was instrumental during the years of the Cold War; it was one of the tools used by Western Europe and the United States to defeat Communism in the former Soviet Block countries.

No one, not our Tinian van drivers, nor our WWII Museum historians, could explain the function of VOA on the island, other than that the towers were "active."

Made me wonder whom we're trying to convert to our current Trumpian way of life.

Guam

The commercial flight from Saipan south to Guam took only twenty-five minutes. Guam is the largest of the Marianas. Marines assaulted the Japanese garrison via Assan and Agat Beaches on the island's west side July 21,1944. Although the Japanese had the defensive advantage of high, very steep terrain, they were reluctant to use their imbedded artillery on the attacking forces below because of the vast numbers of American battleships, cruisers, and destroyers offshore that immediately returned accurate fire on the spot of the artillery flash. Guam was secured after three bloody weeks of battle, including the inevitable banzai charge down the steep terrain above the beaches, but, as always, there were the Japanese who refused to surrender; one stubborn soldier refused to give up until the early 70s!

It was immediately evident that Guam is more prosperous than Saipan. One explanation might be the economic effects of two US bases, one naval and the other air force (B-52 bombers); personnel are currently being shifted to Guam from Okinawa, where the governor and the Japanese prime minister have vowed to remove all US forces. After 73 years it is time.

Maybe it is time to reassess US presence in many of our 800 plus bases around the world.

Iwo Jima

Iwo Jima, meaning "Sulfur Island," was changed back to the original Iwo To (same meaning) by the government of Japan.

I didn't know this until the evening before we left Guam on Saturday, March 24, 2018 for the 73rd Anniversary Ceremony of the Battle of Iwo Jima, attended by both Japanese and Americans, since 1995, called the "Reunion of Honor."

I also didn't know that President Lyndon Johnson returned ownership of Iwo Jima back to the Japanese in 1968, much to the anger and chagrin of many former American combatants.

Who had good reason to be angered and chagrined after the price they paid to capture Iwo: nearly 7,000 killed of nearly 30,000 casualties (Japanese dead numbered 22,000 and 1,000 captured). US planners expected the battle to be won in three days; it lasted more than one month. It was the single bloodiest battle ever fought by the US Marines, who were the majority of the attacking force. Admiral Chester Nimitz, Commander in Chief, Pacific Ocean Areas (CinCPOA), said of the battle, "Uncommon valor was a common occurrence."

Why did President Johnson return the island to Japan? It was mostly a "good will" gesture because Japan had become a strong ally and an important partner in the Pacific. In 1968, Iwo, in 23 years, had lost its strategic importance to US Pacific forces. Also it was very expensive to maintain a defense force there while the Vietnam War was hemorrhaging men and materiel.

The evening before traveling to Iwo and the "Reunion of Honor" an American gentleman who works as the liaison with the Japanese "Reunion" contingent warned our group that we shouldn't expect much in the way of Japanese accommodation for our visit: "If you have the opportunity to ride anywhere, my advice is to take it!"

In other words, we could expect to walk to everything we wanted to see: from the airport hangar to the Reunion ceremony, to the top of Mount Suribachi (where the famous picture of the flag-raisings took place), to the invasion beaches, and return to the hangar: about ten miles total.

Had I fully comprehended this ordeal, I probably would have stayed on Guam. Don't play high school football. Because of one play my senior year, I have had five knee surgeries, including two partial replacements. I simply cannot walk much anymore.

Luckily I caught a ride to the ceremony. Later I hiked to a spot above the invasion beaches to take some pictures, which wasn't easy, as the island, completely denuded from ship and aerial bombardment before and during the assault, resembling a moonscape, is now overgrown with dense grasses, bushes and trees that stand in the way of a good shot. That two plus mile walk was a struggle; I returned as the ceremony was concluding with the wreath-laying, my shirt soaked with sweat, my knees and feet pounding.

The government of Japan only allows American visitors on Iwo one day per year and only for the Reunion of Honor. It is truly a once-in-a-lifetime occasion. As our two chartered 737s left Guam airport we were saluted by a lineup of twenty some United ground personnel, and when we returned two water trucks sprayed our planes, much like a victorious warship returning to home port. While we were on Iwo, USMC personnel handled logistics for American attendees and visitors, having arrived in two C-130 transport planes from Okinawa.

Only a few of our group stayed for the ceremony, mostly the contingent of WWII veterans; the rest were on a mission to climb Suribachi and walk the invasion beaches.

Three large tents surrounded the monument to the Battle of Iwo Jima: one for Americans, one for Japanese officials and visitors, and one on a small hill for the Japanese Army Band that played both American and Japanese military music; also the national anthems of both countries.

Six Japanese officials in funeral garb and two American USMC generals in dress whites spoke while a trio of American women Marines stood at attention, the middle Marine holding aloft the Stars and Stripes, opposite a trio of

Japanese soldiers, the middle one holding the flag of the Rising Sun.

It was very moving. Especially the wreath-laying ceremony by both Japanese and American soldiers.

I admit to getting choked up.

Conclusion

My only response to this incredible trip was, "Wow."

When asked to describe it by those who knew I did this trip, the only word that came to mind was "Vastness."

I really had not prepared myself for the distances involved.

From LAX to Honolulu was six plus hours. From Honolulu to Guam was more than eight hours in a Boeing 777 at 500 plus mph.

The entire time I thought: what was it like to fly this distance in a PB-Y Flying Boat at 100 knots, or even a B-17, capable of little more than 200 plus knots?

Not to mention the men on troop ships, or, worse, the men on "ocean-going" LSTs, puking their guts out for days, weeks, sometimes months, awaiting a beach landing on some island they never heard of.

It is truly amazing that our troops succeeded in all the battles against a fanatical foe that, except on rare occasions, refused surrender.

One of our tour historians, during a lecture on the war in the Pacific, addressed the character of the Japanese soldier, who preferred death, even by ritual suicide, to surrender or capture, which would disgrace his family back home. He explained it in part by citing centuries of Samurai tradition with its code of Bushido, which has many facets, but may best be explained as "the way of the warrior." Bushido does not allow dishonor in any form; surrender or capture is dishonorable.

It is ironic that the spirit of Bushido endured into the twentieth century in spite of the Meiji Restoration, when the Emperor in the late nineteenth/early twentieth centuries was openly pro-Western and did his best to drag Japan into the modern age, after many centuries when it was a closed society. His efforts modernized Japan, especially its weaponry. But not the way its people thought.

"Victory in the Pacific" was way different than the WWII Museum's, "The Rise and Fall of Hitler's Germany" in Germany and Poland, September, 2017.

Different.

But worth it.

I am so glad I did this.

Frankly, I don't ever want to do it again.

I do want to return to the WWII Museum in New Orleans to see the new exhibits that were not ready on my last visit three years ago: "The Road to Tokyo," with a picture of Dad's ship, Bunker Hill, underway after the two Kamikaze attacks during the Battle of Okinawa, and "The Arsenal of Democracy."

Because I have been on, now, two WWII Museum tours, I have a standing invitation to meet with staff in New Orleans for behind-the-scenes looks.

Postscript

I returned to New Orleans the first weekend in May, 2018, spending nearly all of Saturday and Sunday on my own touring the World War II Museum.
On Monday I was first scheduled to meet with two ladies to discuss my desire to sponsor the picture of

Dad's Bunker Hill after the Kamikaze attacks, on display in the Okinawa section of "The Road to Tokyo." I had expressed to them during the "Victory in the Pacific" tour what I had in mind...that is, if I could afford it. They burst my bubble almost immediately by telling me individual pictures are no longer allowed to be sponsored, as that can detract from a visitor's experience (which makes sense). They also informed me the Okinawa exhibit was already co-sponsored, in part funded by a Mr. Drew Brees, the quarterback of the New Orleans Saints pro football team (he has more money than I). They did offer a couple of suggestions as to how I could commemorate Dad's service: we'll see.

After the meeting I was given a "Docent Tour" with a WWII Museum volunteer historian of the "Road to Tokyo," which was most interesting, even though I had toured it on my own on Saturday. He pointed out a map (that I had missed) of all the Japanese cities that had been fire bombed by B-29s dropping incendiary bombs from low altitude, the per-cent of their destruction, with a population comparison of those cities with comparable cities in the United States at the time. These bombing raids killed and wounded far more civilians than the two atomic bombs dropped on Hiroshima and Nagasaki.

We then joined James L, Museum Curator, for a behind the scenes look at some of the vaults where donated items are stored that are not on display in the museum; we had to don plastic gloves to handle anything James handed us: uniforms, weapons, medical kits, and medals, including one commemorating the July 20, 1944, assassination attempt on Adolph Hitler at the Wolfsschanze, the war bunker in what is now northern Poland...that medal was probably owned by Hitler himself, as it was found by an American soldier in

Hitler's writing desk in the Chancellery after the fall of Berlin.

James also showed us an American Purple Heart medal, awarded those wounded in battle, that was produced, among many thousands of others, for Operation Downfall, the planned invasion of the Japanese home islands by American armed forces to end the war in the Pacific. The expectation was that our forces would suffer upwards of a million casualties confronting soldiers, but also civilians -- men, women, and children -- armed with sharpened bamboo pikes, on the beaches; everyone Japanese would be the enemy.

Dropping the atomic bombs convinced one person that Japan must surrender: Emperor Hirohito, who made a recording, broadcast to the nation, that Japan "...must endure the unendurable."

Thus the bombs, which killed and maimed hundreds of thousands, saved the lives of hundreds of thousands, if not millions, on both sides.

James told us something I will never forget: Purple Heart medals awarded in every war since WWII -- Korea, Vietnam, Desert Storm, Afghanistan, and Iraq -- came from the inventory of those medals produced for Operation Downfall.

RIVER CRUISE AND TOUR OF PORTUGAL AND SPAIN, APRIL 2018

This was our first ever river cruise and we began it full of expectations. Plus neither of us had ever visited Portugal.

From Bismarck to Lisbon, Portugal: three planes, Bismarck-Minneapolis, Minneapolis-Paris (Charles de Gaulle), CDG-Lisbon: 16 hours en route.

We arrived at our downtown Lisbon Hotel, The Corinthia, and promptly crashed from the after effects of having taken an Ambien sleeping tablet for the over-Atlantic portion of the trip.

Ambien is truly a wonder drug. Taken after several alcoholic drinks (your doctor will NOT recommend this), it cuts the length of the trip by hours, thereby overcoming jet lag. Arrive in Europe having slept; don't sleep until at least 10 PM, and, next morning, you are good to go.

No Ambien: you are condemned to days of fitful sleep/insomnia to overcome jet lag.

BUT! With Ambien you run the risk of arriving so sleepy in Europe, that all you want to do is sleep. Why you need to take two Ambien, the second before falling asleep for the night in your hotel: the next morning you will be ready to go.

After a nap, and some recuperating time in the hotel bar, my wife, Maryvonne, and I crossed the rainy street in Lisbon to Restaurant "Sete Mares," (Seven Seas), which was recommended by our hotel barman as "Muit Boa," Muy Bueno, Tres Bon, Excellent!

No matter the language, he was on target.

We ordered Cataplana, a typical Portuguese kind of bouillabaisse, with a Portuguese greenish white wine, meaning dry, a perfect fit with fish/seafood.

Steaming palourds, langoustines, crawfish, potatoes, onions, and sliced peppers in a reddish sauce greeted our eyes and nostrils when our waiter pulled back the copper top. It was a kaleidoscope of delectability.

Our waiter spoke Portuguese, Spanish, French, and English. Maryvonne told him, "C'est comme le petit Jesus en culotte de velours." (Like Jesus in velvet pants).

He agreed.

Be Careful What You Wish For

That was the first day.

Things went downhill from there.

First, I caught a horrible chest cold, and was constantly coughing and blowing my running faucet of a nose. Then it became cool and rainy. And our hotel was far from downtown, accessible only by bus or cab (we wondered why?). Outside of a couple of restaurants the only thing of interest nearby was a multi-story, high-end department store.

We had paid for a luxury cruise on the Douro River, but our first two days were spent in a bus: first a tour of historic Lisbon, then the drive the next day to the city of Porto, in northern Portugal. After a tour there, we were to embark on Uniworld Boutique River Cruises', Queen Isabela.

Our vivacious, knowledgeable lady guide, Sofie, explained that Lisbon is pronounced "Leezhboah" in Portuguese. It is a mix of very ancient, old, classic, and dumpy modern, especially the ubiquitous newer apartment buildings.

Except for bus rides to drop-off points, the tour consisted of our group traipsing behind Sofie, with her raised #1 group sign, to visit various sites in the historic port area, a famous pastry shop, and, inevitably, the cathedral (My opinion: see one cathedral, you've seen 'em all).

Maryvonne, my French wife, and I had the same thought: we had turned into Japanese tourists.

Or, worse: Tante Agnes.

Tante (Aunt) Agnes, was Maryvonne's second cousin; nobody has ever explained how she came to be Tante Agnes. She was never anyone's aunt.

Tante Agnes was a buxom lady with extremely large, overflowing breasts, who maintained a running commentary on anything and everything. She was very dramatic in voice and gestures, constantly enhancing images with grand sweeps of her arms.

Every summer Tante Agnes participated in an organized bus

tour with 40-50 other French blue hairs of a European country outside of France.

Every time I saw her I made a point of asking her about her latest trip.

Usually it started like this: "D'abord, pour-quoi tout le monde ne parle pas la meme langue?!" "Why doesn't everyone speak the same language?!" Meaning French, of course. What else?

"Qu'est-ce qu'on a mal mange!" "How badly we ate!"

"Les choses absolument affreuses!" "Horrible things!"

"Et leur vin…de la piquette!" "And their wine…swill!"

Tantes Agnes was talking about Italy, Spain, and Portugal.

I counseled her NEVER to travel to Germany or England; the human race could ill-afford WWIII, and

England and France did not want a renewal of the Hundred Years War.

Maryvonne and I had decided at a young age never to turn into blue hair bus tourists.

But there we were.

A Change in the Weather

We were both a bit disheartened and disappointed, especially when we arrived in Porto, only to find out that our ship was blocked upstream by fast-running water through the locks, the result of spring rains in Spain; we would have to spend the night in a hotel in Porto.

Oh, well.

But the next day dawned with a brilliant sun, blue skies, and a hint of warming temperatures, cheering everyone.

Kind of reminded me of Alan Sherman's song when I was a teenager:

Hello Muddah, hello Faddah
Here I am at Camp Grenada
Camp is very entertaining
And they say we'll have some fun if it stops raining

I went hiking with Joe Spivey
He developed poison ivy
You remember Leonard skinner
He got Ptomaine poisoning last night after dinner...

Take me home, oh Muddah, Faddah
Take me home, I hate Grenada
Don't leave me out in the forest where
I might get eaten by a bear...

Wait a minute, its stopped hailing
Guys are swimming, guys are sailing
Playing baseball, gee that's bettah
Muddah, Faddah kindly disregard this letter

The Portuguese

Beginning in the early fifteenth century and into the sixteenth and seventeenth, the unexplored world outside Europe became Portugal's oyster. The world was hers to be taken. Not since the Romans had a country traveled to such distant lands as did the explorers of Portugal. Tiny, insignificant Portugal, of all the unlikely countries of Europe! A century before its kings were so destitute they couldn't even mint currency. By the latter part of the sixteenth it had become the richest country on Earth.

All this stemming from a bold love of adventure as well as the desire for riches. Fortunes and human lives were risked. The average sailing took two years, during which time it was routine for the crew to lose two-thirds of its complement, mostly to diseases such as scurvy and beriberi.

Alas. Since that Golden Age of Discovery, Portugal has "...been riding at anchor," as described by one writer. It is a member of the EU, but it's one of the poorest members, subsidized by its larger, more prosperous neighbors.

During my stay I couldn't figure out Portugal or the Portuguese, whom I would describe as "swarthy," like they all descended from hard working peasant stock. They and their country didn't appear rich, but, then, neither did they seem poor. Most apartment buildings are new or newer. The people seem content, if not outright happy. They seem stuck, but contentedly so, in what former dictator, Antonio Salazar, referred to as the Portuguese triptych: "Fado" (traditional folkloric music), football (the opiate of the people), and Fatima (the lingering influence of the Catholic Church.)

Maybe it is socialism, that word so misunderstood in the US, even though much of our economy and infrastructure are the result of a sharing of resources and taxes. It was explained to us that the Portuguese government reduces the onus on individuals by taxing everything at high rates to pay for universal health care, education, and retirement. Say what you will; it is one way a poor country can provide its citizens a measure of quality of life.

Our River Cruise is Spent Mostly in Hotels and Buses

What was supposed to be our second night on the cruise ship, we again passed in a hotel.

We finally joined our ship in the pretty little Douro River town, Pinhao, in the heart of Port wine country, and about half way on our initial cruise itinerary. Finally underway, I sat on the top deck and marveled at the steep slopes rising from the river banks, covered in terraces of vines that had to have taken years, if not centuries, of back-breaking manual labor to create.

The ship was blocked at the downstream lock by high water turbulence; we returned to Pinhao for the night.

The next morning, with the river still blocked from navigation, we boarded a bus for the steep, serpentine climb up a vine-terraced mountain to the Sandeman Port Wine Vineyard, begun in 1790 by a Scotsman, George Sandeman. It is now owned by a conglomerate, which also owns other former family wine estates.

The Romans were originally attracted to this area because of its mini-climate, conducive to wine production – hot, sunny summers and mild, wet and snowy winters.

As we learned at Sandeman's and, again, the next day, at the Port Wine Museum in Regua, downstream from Pinhao, because our ship was again blocked between impassable locks, Douro wine growers soon discovered that this mini climate produced grapes with high sugar, hence high-alcohol content. When fortified with distilled spirits, the result is port: a wine with a heavier, velvety texture, 19-20% alcohol, that can keep, under proper conditions, for years; in fact, most vintages only improve with age. Sweeter ports go well with desserts or pungent cheeses like Roquefort. Drier versions make delicious aperitifs that prepare the palate for what is to follow.

A lecturer at the Port Wine Museum showed slides that depicted the labor-intensive nature of this business. Almost nothing involves modern machinery: from stacking slate rocks to build terraces, planting vines, pruning them, picking the grapes, then pruning the vines for winter. The only part of wine making that has been taken over by machines: crushing the grapes, which used to be done by teams of men walking bare legged in vats. And there are millions if not tens of millions of individual vine plants in the region!

After two attempts at the lock upstream, our captain gave up; it was simply too risky to go on. We spent two more nights docked at Pinhao.

The last day we received a letter of apology from Uniworld, placed on our bed, for our "inconvenience and disappointment," offering us $1,000 each as a credit on our next Uniworld cruise.

Most of us threw this in "File 13," as the cruise cost $14,000 for two passengers.

A lousy $1,000 for not doing what we expected…and paid for?

And there was great understanding among the passengers about river conditions, which Uniworld, nor any of the other cruise companies could control.

Someone must have really complained: the day I returned home to Bismarck, North Dakota, the offer got upped to $2,500; the next day it was $3,500.

As the Mexicans say, "Vamos a ver:" "We shall see."

On to Spain and Madrid

The last night that should have passed on the riverboat we spent in a hotel in Northeastern Portugal with a really crummy restaurant. The next morning we headed for Salamanca and Madrid, Spain by bus.

Salamanca is known as the "Golden City," because of its white limestone that turns to a golden hue as it ages. With overcast skies we had to trust our guide's statement that the golden effect is most pronounced in the late afternoon sun.

What I didn't believe was his statement that the statue in the middle of an intersection was that of Don Quixote astride his horse, Rosinante. Whoever paid for this statue should demand that the money be repaid. The statue depicts a muscular man on an equally muscular horse, sans lance in hand.

The "real" Don Quixote was a broken down, old, crazy man who rode a broken down nag and constantly carried a broken down lance.

Avila

On the bus ride to Madrid we had a pee stop outside the medieval fortress city, Avila, made famous by St. Theresa of Avila, who proclaimed that she was the reincarnation of Jesus...and, apparently, she was believed, according to the plaque facing the fortress across a river. The plaque claimed she is considered a pillar of the Roman Catholic Church.

Really?

If someone claimed today to be the reincarnation of Jesus, either she would be inundated by donations from non-thinking believers, or she would be condemned as a charlatan. Either way she would become very wealthy. Too bad for Theresa of Avila that she was born before her time; she died a penniless nun.

Madrid

Although I had visited Madrid two years earlier, the first morning I just had to go on the organized bus tour, mostly for the Prado Museum, to see once again the painting by Velasquez, "Las Meninas," which Pablo Picasso, who reproduced it in multiple cubist renderings, called, "La Pintura." Velasquez was the court painter for King Philip IV. "Las Meninas" is, ostensibly, a painting of the Infanta, Margaret Theresa, and her entourage of ladies in waiting. But it includes Velasquez painting the scene; in his rear are the King and Queen and a gentleman standing in a doorway. The painting is, in fact, a study in perspective, perhaps one of the most outstanding in the history of painting: why Picasso called it "<u>The</u> Painting."

Also not to be missed are the areas dedicated to El Greco and Goya.

But that is all of the Prado that you will want to see, or will have the time or the stamina to see. The Prado is the largest collection of art in the entire world. There is more art that is not displayed than is on display. Plus the crowds are crushing.

Flamenco Dinner and Dance Show

Does a dance exist that is more flamboyant, fluid, and hypnotic than Flamenco?

Two years prior to this trip I visited Madrid with another tour group and we were bussed to a dinner/Flamenco dance club, where a young woman dancer explained to us the origins of Flamenco: probably Gypsy from the southern part of Spain – Andalusia, Extremadura, and Murcia. Now danced to guitar accompaniment, Flamenco originally was called "toque de palmas," "clapping of hands" and singing.

The popularity of Flamenco has spread through the years. We were told the best Flamenco shows in Spain are now found in Madrid. But it has a worldwide appeal. During the Q & A with the young woman dancer someone said, 'I detect an accent." To which she replied, "I'm Australian."

Our Duoro River cruise group was crammed tightly into a smallish restaurant with a tiny, wooden dance floor; Maryvonne and I sat across from one another, next to the floor, which was about eye level. The "dinner" consisted of a sampling of Spanish delicacies, accompanied by white and red wines. We weren't there to "fill up," but to take in the show, which started promptly at 8:00 PM with two guitarists who first "warmed us up" with Flamenco music.

Two men and a woman danced individually throughout the performance, which was not only mesmerizing, but cacophonous to us seated so close to the pounding of their shoes; we could feel the intensity in our bodies.

The woman, a brunette with steely blue eyes, riveted to a spot across the restaurant, danced with such ferocity that she seemed virtually alone on stage, in spite of the strumming guitarists and the two male dancers who clapped their hands in rhythm.

The second man, shorter but very muscular, danced so hard that he soon was covered in beads of sweat, which showered down on us seated next to the stage.

An evening not to forget, which none of us wanted to end.

The Heart of Madrid

What I think I like best about Madrid is that it is very "walkable."

Most of the sites worth visiting are within walking distance. And, if you have bad knees as I do, if the distance is a bit far, there are hundreds of sidewalk bars and cafes where one can stop for a beer or glass of wine or a local dish, such as a deep-fried calamari sandwich, or, my fave, morcilla (pronounced mor-see-ja), sliced blood sausage.

My favorite sites include:

The Plaza Mayor, a huge square surrounded by seventeenth century buildings three stories tall, which is the social gathering place of Madrid. The four sides are lined with outdoor cafes; the bottom floors of the buildings contain all kinds of shops, and the center of the square is populated by performers, musicians, and even a fat Spider Man (for pictures), all trying to earn a little extra money.

The Mercado de San Miguel, a nineteenth century building with wrought iron columns located about a block from The Plaza Mayor, that contains the most wondrous collection of stalls of gourmet delights that I have ever seen in one location: sausages, beers, sea food, desserts, wines, meats, cheeses, candies, liquors...you name it, it is all there. Only problem: want to sample any of it, you will have to eat at the counter while standing.

Puerto del Sol: Madrid's place to rendezvous and demonstrate against anything that bothers you. Also "Kilometer Zero" for the national roads that radiate out of Madrid to the rest of Spain.

Reina Sofia Museum, the modern art museum, which contains Picasso's huge painting,

"Guernica," his rendition of the bombing of innocent elderly men, and women and children in the town of the same name in northern Spain by the German Condor Legion during the Spanish Civil War, fought prior to WWII.

Museo Thyssen-Bournemisza, which I visited for the first time on the Duoro River trip. In many ways I like this museum better than The Prado; for one thing, there are fewer visitors. The Thyssen contains one of the most important private collections of art ever assembled, sold to Spain in 1993. The story has it that Baron Heinrich Thyssen-Bournemisza and his son began buying art that reflected the different European styles through the centuries. Later, the Baron's beautiful young wife, Carmen (large paintings of each greet the visitor at the museum entrance) added many Impressionist and modern paintings. In a word, the collection is "eclectic," from Rembrandt, Titian, Goya, Picasso, Van Gogh...to even one Charlie Russell Painting of an Indian attack in the nineteenth century near his home of Great Falls, Montana.

Conclusion

In retrospect this wasn't as bad a trip as it was working up to be. Granted, it would have been more fun and interesting to see the sites of the Duoro River by riverboat rather than by bus. But one cannot control the weather, the "force majeure" of travel.

Portugal is now in my "bucket," the forty-first foreign country I have visited (Plus all fifty of the United States).

And through the belated generosity of Uniworld Boutique Cruises, we now have enough credit to pay for one person's fare on a future river cruise. Except I have already alerted our travel agent to look for one that has the fewest excursions requiring travel by bus.

MY ULTIMATE BUCKET LIST WISH

Well...to get this book published for anyone who might be interested before I "tip over."

Maybe I should title this chapter "My Penultimate Bucket Wish List."

As I write this I am 71 years of age. I don't know how many more "Bucket List" wishes remain that I can fulfill.

In truth, except for conducting a symphony orchestra and driving a Porsche as fast as I could, I have never really had a "Bucket List" of things I have wanted to do.

Most things have just kind of come my way.

I am ok with that.

May more things come to me before I "tip over." Stay tuned.